Habeas Corpus: A Very Short Introduction

Very Short Introductions available now:

Available soon:

PHILOSOPHY OF MIND
    Barbara Gail Montero
BLASPHEMY Yvonne Sherwood

PAKISTAN Pippa Virdee
TIME Jenann Ismael
JAMES JOYCE Colin MacCabe

For more information visit our website

www.oup.com/vsi/

Amanda L. Tyler

HABEAS CORPUS

A Very Short Introduction

OXFORD
UNIVERSITY PRESS

OXFORD
UNIVERSITY PRESS

Oxford University Press is a department of the University of Oxford.
It furthers the University's objective of excellence in research, scholarship,
and education by publishing worldwide. Oxford is a registered trade mark of
Oxford University Press in the UK and certain other countries.

Published in the United States of America by Oxford University Press
198 Madison Avenue, New York, NY 10016, United States of America.

Library of Congress Cataloging-in-Publication Data
Names: Tyler, Amanda L., author.
Title: Habeas corpus : a very short introduction / Amanda L. Tyler.
Description: New York : Oxford University Press, 2021. | Series: Very short
introduction | Includes bibliographical references and index.
Identifiers: LCCN 2021004466 | ISBN 9780190918989 (paperback) |
ISBN 9780190919009 (epub)
Subjects: LCSH: Habeas corpus. | Habeas corpus—Great Britain—History. |
Habeas corpus—United States—History.
Classification: LCC K5453 .T95 2021 | DDC 345.73/056—dc23
LC record available at https://lccn.loc.gov/2021004466

1 3 5 7 9 8 6 4 2

Printed in Great Britain by Ashford Colour Press Ltd., Gosport, Hants.

For my parents

Contents

List of illustrations

Habeas Corpus

Acknowledgments

I owe tremendous thanks and appreciation to a host of persons who helped me with the research that went into the preparation of this book. The list includes the extraordinary librarians at the University of California, Berkeley School of Law Library, and most especially Ellen Gilmore, Marci Hoffman, Michael Levy, Edna Lewis, and I-Wei Wang. I am likewise in debt to the librarians and archivists who assisted me in my research on-site at Lincoln's Inn, the British Library, the British National Archives, the British Parliamentary Archives, and the Library of Congress.

This project has benefited from countless conversations with colleagues at Berkeley Law and other schools. The same is true with respect to the exceptional work of a host of former research assistants who engaged in research for antecedent and related projects, as well as the more recent assistance of Djenab Conde (Berkeley Law '19), Lana El-Farra (Berkeley Law '20), Ashley Johnson (Berkeley Law '21), Jennifer Lee (Dartmouth College '22), Jonathan Rosenthal (Berkeley Law '19), Carmen Sobczak (Berkeley Law '21), and Jordan Varberg (Berkeley Law '19), who helped me usher this particular project to fruition. My thinking on this project likewise had been advanced as a result of discussions and debates with my fantastic students at Berkeley, especially those in my Federal Courts classes and my seminar on the Constitution in Wartime. To all, I am deeply grateful.

I am indebted to the anonymous outside reviewers on both the proposal and an early draft of the manuscript for their very helpful feedback and suggestions for ways to expand the reach of the book.

Special thanks are owed to Nancy Toff of Oxford University Press for her patience and exceptional assistance in ushering this book from inception to publication.

Finally, as always, I owe my greatest appreciation to my spouse and my children, who have always been at the ready to cheer on my efforts and support me in countless ways in my work.

Introduction

The storied writ of habeas corpus—literally, to hold the body—has enjoyed celebrated status in the common law tradition for centuries. Writing in the eighteenth century, the widely influential English jurist and commentator William Blackstone once labeled the writ of habeas corpus a "bulwark of our liberties." Soon thereafter, a member of Parliament glorified the writ as the "great palladium of the liberties of the subject." Meanwhile, across the Atlantic, in the lead-up to the American Revolution, the Continental Congress declared that the habeas privilege and the right to trial by jury were among the most important rights in a free society, "without which a people cannot be free and happy." A few years later, while promoting the ratification of the US Constitution in *The Federalist*, Alexander Hamilton celebrated the privilege as one of the "greate[st] securities to liberty and republicanism" known. Thus, as another participant in the ratification debates stated, the writ of habeas corpus has long been viewed as "essential to freedom."

Legend ties the origins of the writ of habeas corpus to Magna Carta—the "Great Charter of the Liberties of England"—sealed by King John on a field at Runnymede in 1215. Chapter 39 of the Great Charter declared, "No free man shall be taken or imprisoned or dispossessed, or outlawed, or banished, or in any way destroyed, nor will we go upon him, nor send upon him, except by the legal judgment of his peers or by the law of the land."

The Charter, which emerged from a period of great unrest in England, represented a bargain of sorts between rebelling English nobility and King John, who remained in power in exchange for recognizing the liberties set forth in the compact. The concept of due process, so foundational to the jurisprudence of individual liberty throughout the common law tradition, traces its roots directly to Chapter 39.

In the seventeenth century, when the modern law of habeas corpus came into its own, the great English jurist and commentator Sir Edward Coke connected Chapter 39 with the writ of habeas corpus in his widely read *Institutes on the Law of England*. There, he declared, "Now it may be demanded, if a man be taken, or committed to prison *contra legem terrae*, against the law of the land, what remedy hath the party grieved?" To this, he answered, "He may have an *habeas corpus*." In Coke's vision, the writ empowers courts to ensure that no one is deprived of liberty in violation of "the law of the land."

The writ of habeas corpus at the center of this story is the writ *ad subjiciendum et recipiendum*, which translates loosely as "to undergo and receive" the *corpus*—or body—of the prisoner. Through issuance of the writ, courts take jurisdiction over the prisoner and demand that the relevant custodian (typically the jailor) present legal cause for the prisoner's detention. As Chief Justice Coke explained while presiding over a habeas case in the Court of King's Bench, "By the law of God, none ought to be imprisoned, but with the cause expressed." In classic habeas procedure, the court took jurisdiction over the prisoner by bringing the prisoner physically into court and then ordered that the jailor proffer what was known as a "return" setting forth the basis for the detention. In practice, common law courts have used other writs of habeas corpus to compel the appearance of witnesses, move prisoners, and demand responses in civil proceedings. These examples highlight the expansive range of use of habeas in the common law tradition.

From its origins in English law, it took little time for the writ of habeas corpus *ad subjiciendum et recipiendum* to take flight, following the common law to the outer reaches of the British Empire. In the early twenty-first century, this concept of habeas corpus may be found embedded in legal traditions throughout the former empire as well as in jurisdictions whose legal frameworks draw influence from those countries in turn. One prominent example on this list is, of course, the United States of America. Many additional jurisdictions likewise enjoy a habeas privilege that is the product of Anglo-American influence. To name but a few, the list includes Australia, Canada, India, Ireland, Israel, Barbados, the Republic of Korea, South Africa, and New Zealand. More generally, the principles at the core of the habeas privilege have made their way into international law, including Article 5 of the European Convention on Human Rights.

At its inception, the concept of habeas corpus was inextricably intertwined with the role of the judge. Judges, after all, were at the center of the common law tradition and created and wielded the writ for many purposes. Notwithstanding what Blackstone and others would have us believe, however, judicial authority to employ the writ derived initially not from a special calling to preside over the liberty of the subject. Instead, at its origins, habeas corpus was a prerogative writ—a writ pursuant to which a court exercised the authority of the monarch—empowering the royal courts to act on behalf of the king in "demand[ing an] account for his subject who is restrained of his liberty."

Important developments in the story of the writ of habeas corpus occurred in England during the latter part of the seventeenth century in the period leading up to and following the Glorious Revolution. It was here, as part of the rise of parliamentary supremacy, that the writ finally trained its focus on the king and acted to limit his powers. In the lead-up to this period, the common law writ had failed to check summary executive detention at the hands of the increasingly tyrannical Charles I. This proved one of many reasons that Charles lost his head in front of the Banqueting House, launching the English Civil War and the Interregnum period during which England abandoned the monarchy. With the restoration of the monarchy in 1660, Parliament left little to chance, taking more and more power for itself. Thus, among many other things, Parliament adopted the English Habeas Corpus Act of 1679 and took control of the law governing executive detention as well as the judges charged with overseeing the same. Specifically, through the act, Parliament employed the royal courts and the common law writ as vehicles for limiting the power of the executive to detain outside the criminal process. In so doing, Parliament imposed substantial constraints on the executive, even in the most serious of cases— those involving suspected traitors. As history unfolded, events confirmed that the act governed even in wartime and even in the face of serious threats to the throne that followed the Glorious Revolution. It was only by suspending the protections of the Habeas Corpus Act, which Parliament did for the first time in 1689 at the request of the new king, William, that the protections of the act came to be displaced and Parliament empowered the executive to arrest and detain persons suspected of posing a threat to the state on suspicion alone.

It is from this period that the English Habeas Corpus Act came to be viewed as an enormously significant constraint on executive power and widely championed as one of the most important protections of individual liberty. Thus, for example, in the widely read 1765 publication of his law lectures—lectures that were read by virtually every early American studying law—William Blackstone glorified the Habeas Corpus Act as nothing less than a "second *magna carta*." Another prominent treatise on English law written by Henry Care and studied by early Americans championed the act as going further than the common law writ to ensure that so-called state prisoners would no longer languish in the Tower of London on a king's whim. No doubt influenced by these and other sources on English law, the American founding generation came likewise to view the protections associated with the Habeas Corpus Act as "essential to freedom."

This Very Short Introduction will tell the story of what is sometimes known as "the Great Writ" as it has unfolded in Anglo-American law. The primary jurisdictions explored will be Great Britain and the United States, but many aspects of this story will ring familiar to those in other countries with a robust habeas tradition. Along the way, the book will chronicle the long-standing role of the common law writ as a vehicle for reviewing detentions for conformity with underlying law, as well as more specifically the profound influence of the English Habeas Corpus Act of 1679 on Anglo-American law. The book will highlight how under certain circumstances the common law writ has come up short. It will also, however, tell stories of how on other occasions the common law writ has proved immensely significant in the story of individual liberty, including, to offer but one example, as a vehicle for freeing slaves.

The pages that follow also explore the English Habeas Corpus Act and its importance in Anglo-American habeas jurisprudence, including its enormous influence on the drafting of the US Constitution. They also will reveal the waning influence of the act in the twentieth and twenty-first centuries. It is during this period that courts in both countries moved away from a suspension model grounded in the act's protections and—sometimes for better and sometimes for worse—embraced a vision of habeas drawing primarily on the common law writ, heralding its adaptability to address new circumstances as they arise, but sometimes doing so at the expense of the core protections enshrined in and long associated with the Habeas Corpus Act.

In the United States, unlike in Great Britain, "the privilege of the writ of habeas corpus" is protected in a written constitution. Specifically, the privilege is protected from suspension "unless when in Cases of Rebellion or Invasion the public Safety may require it." Nonetheless, in both the United States and Great Britain, which does not formally have a codified constitution, the development of habeas jurisprudence has proceeded along similar trajectories. In both countries, habeas jurisprudence encountered similar and at times overwhelming pressure during the world wars of the twentieth century and the threat of terrorism that came later, and that pressure to yield to the asserted needs of the state at the expense of individual liberty resulted in the prioritization of national security above all else. Accordingly, the story told here is not one in which the writ of habeas corpus has always deserved the accolades that Blackstone and others have heaped upon it. It is instead a story that reveals more generally the pressures that war, among other things, places on legal constraints and constitutional values, along with how difficult it is for those constraints and values to stand inviolate in all times. But, as will be seen, there are also chapters of the story chronicled here that reveal just how powerful the writ can be in checking executive power and championing individual liberty. This story, in other words, is one that reveals both the potential and the limits of the so-called Great Writ.

Chapter 1
The English origins

In the early twenty-first century, the concept of habeas corpus is understood to mean many things. In the United States, for example, the concept has become practically synonymous with additional layers of review of criminal convictions. Likewise, habeas corpus is the means by which many immigration matters come before the courts. But if we trace its origins to the early seventeenth century, we find that the common law writ was born out of a simple idea—the need to serve the king. Royal courts employed the writ as a vehicle for acting on behalf of the king to demand justification for the detention of one of his subjects. Given that the royal courts were in the service of the king during this period, it makes sense that there was little reason for those courts to question the king himself. And until the seventeenth century, the king as sovereign could claim to be the source of all law. Put more simply, he could do no wrong. All of this changed over the course of the seventeenth century, but it took time and much strife.

Consider the case of the Five Knights, sometimes called Darnel's case, from 1627. Charles I, whose execution launched the English Civil War, was often at odds with his Parliament. When that body cut off funding for the king's plans to continue fighting the Thirty Years' War, he turned to a number of wealthy nobles for financial support. The five knights at the center of Darnel's case refused the king's entreaties. He therefore ordered them arrested and detained at London's Fleet Prison. Represented by some of the English bar's finest lawyers, the nobles petitioned the Court of King's Bench, the judges of which served at the pleasure of the king, for writs of habeas corpus to win their release. When the court requested that the Crown justify the detentions in a return, as the responsive pleading in habeas cases is known, Attorney General Robert Heath stated nothing more than that the prisoners were held "per speciale mandatum Domini Regis"—that is, by the special command of the king. Did this alone provide sufficient legal justification for their detention?

The knights' counsel, which included the celebrated parliamentarian, lawyer, and legal scholar John Selden, attacked the position that the royal command alone constituted the law of the land, or *legem terrae* in the language of Magna Carta. Selden argued, "The law saith expressly, 'No freeman shall be imprisoned without due process of the law.'" Due process, Selden contended, encompassed "due course of law, to be either by presentment or by indictment." Thus, Selden equated due process with full-scale criminal prosecution. Given that the knights had not been charged with any crime, Selden argued that the court should set them free.

Heath countered that any definition of *legem terrae* must recognize that the "king is the head of the same fountain of justice, which your lordship administers to all his subjects; all justice is derived from him." In other words, what the king declares is law, plain and simple. This meant that the king had the power to detain any prisoner for so-called state reasons.

In the end, the Crown prevailed. Although it recognized the momentousness of the case, the Court of King's Bench would not question the king's authority to detain by his own command, concluding consistent with contemporary understanding that the king was the source of all law. Instead, the court told the prisoners that to win their freedom, their only option was to ask the king for "mercy."

Given that the Court of King's Bench believed that it was not for the courts to question the king's jurisdiction over matters of state, when studied in context, the case of the Five Knights is not especially noteworthy. But because of both the breadth of the power to detain that it recognized and the temper of the times, in short order the decision launched a decades-long effort to limit the scope of executive detention. Events began immediately following the case, when John Selden partnered with fellow member of Parliament Sir Edward Coke, who had returned to politics after being dismissed as chief justice of the Court of King's Bench. Together, the two promoted the Petition of Right in Parliament to rebuke the decision against the knights and more broadly question the king's unlimited discretion over matters of state security.

For his part, Coke emphasized the dangers of unlimited executive power to detain while contending that "Magna Carta and other statutes" *already* denied the king the power to detain for unilaterally asserted "state reasons": "We cannot yield to this, that [the King] should have power to commit any, and within 'convenient time' he shall declare the cause;... if it be *per mandatum domini regis*, or 'for matter of state';... then we are gone, and we are in a worse case than ever. If we agree to this imprisonment 'for matters of state' and 'a convenient time,' we shall leave Magna Carta and the other statutes and make them fruitless, and do what our ancestors would never do." Parliament adopted the Petition of Right in 1628, just one year after the case of the Five Knights.

In its final form, the petition quoted Chapter 39 of Magna Carta and set forth the following grievance and demand:

> Your subjects have of late been imprisoned without any cause
> shewed: And when for their deliverance they were brought before
> your justices by your Majesties writts of habeas corpus...no cause
> was certified, but that they were deteined by your Majesties speciall
> comaund signified by the lords of your privie councell, and yet were
> returned backe to severall prisons without being charged with any
> thing to which they might make aunswere according to the
> lawe....They...pray...that no freeman in any such manner as is
> before mencioned be imprisoned or deteined.

The petition was a stark rebuke of the reasoning of the Court of King's Bench in the case of the Five Knights, and it also purported to restrict declarations of martial law, ban forced quartering of soldiers, and prohibit unilateral taxation by the king. It marked in this respect an important turning point in the power struggles between Parliament and the monarchy that came to define much of seventeenth-century England.

In its immediate wake, the petition changed little on the ground, in part because of its debatable legal status. Indeed, only one year later, Charles I threw John Selden and eight other members of Parliament into the Tower of London in 1629 for their open opposition to his actions. Selden and the other prisoners went before King's Bench to seek their freedom via writs of habeas corpus, arguing in reliance on the petition that the king could not detain them outside the criminal process. Once again, the arguments came up short, though they did garner some traction. Records from this period suggest that the justices of King's Bench were inclined to side with the prisoners. When they wrote to the king to inform him of this fact, he responded by moving the prisoners to the Tower of London and refusing to submit them to the court's jurisdiction, leading King's Bench never to announce its opinion in the case.

Nonetheless, in questioning the unchecked discretion of the king over matters of state, the petition set in motion important developments in English habeas law. In 1641, Parliament dissolved the "Court commonly called the Star Chamber" and declared that any person imprisoned by the king or his close advisers, including those who served on the Privy Council, had the right to challenge a detention through a writ of habeas corpus before the Court of King's Bench or Common Pleas. The act required judges to "examine and determine whether the cause of...commitment appearing upon the...return be just and legall." Finally, to enforce its mandate that the jailor be bound to make a return justifying the detention, the law provided that anyone acting "contrary to the direction and true meaning" of the act could be ordered to pay the prisoner treble damages. Parliament had begun the process of instituting statutory limitations on executive detention, but it was not until after the English Civil War that the aspirations of Selden and Cook finally took hold.

In the meantime, those in power increasingly employed the practice of sending prisoners to "legal islands"—whether true islands or the Tower of London—to escape the reach of writs of habeas corpus. During this period, the failings of the judicially created common law writ of habeas corpus to check this practice and other abuses became increasingly apparent. In 1667, for example, the House of Commons began impeachment proceedings against the Earl of Clarendon for his role in sending prisoners to "remote islands, garrisons, and other places, thereby to prevent them from the benefit of the law." Meanwhile, the Commons also criticized the chief justice of the Court of King's Bench, Sir John Kelyng, for denying habeas to a state prisoner who had spent five years in the tower based solely on an order from the king's advisers. These and other examples lay bare the fact that while the royal courts were under the control of the Crown, the common law writ of habeas corpus could only do so much.

Accordingly, in 1679, Parliament finally passed legislation that both limited dramatically the power of the executive to detain and compelled the courts to implement the law's mandates under threat of penalty. With the English Habeas Corpus Act of 1679, Parliament took control over the law of detention and habeas corpus jurisprudence entered a new chapter.

Parliament's objectives in passing the Habeas Corpus Act sprang from its intention to expand its power at the expense of the king much more so than from a desire to protect individual liberty. The act must therefore be understood as part of the rise of parliamentary supremacy that occurred during this period and the larger movement away from royal absolutism. Underscoring this point, after the act's adoption, Parliament continued to wield its attainder power to circumvent the act and summarily order the imprisonment and punishment of individuals without any judicial process whatsoever, a practice difficult to reconcile with any narrative that paints Parliament during this period as a great champion of individual liberty. Only ten years after passing the act, moreover, Parliament invented the concept of suspension to set aside the act's protections to protect the state.

Even when understood in context, the English Habeas Corpus Act accomplished a great deal. It dramatically constrained executive detention, effectively eliminating the concept of a "state prisoner"—that is, a prisoner detained by the executive solely on suspicion. (Only when subsequently authorized by an act of suspension could the Crown detain once again on such terms.) The act did so by taking control of the royal courts and commanding them to do its bidding under threat of penalty. The houses entitled the legislation "An Act for the better securing the Liberty of the Subject, and for preventing of Imprisonments beyond the Seas." In setting out the act's terms, Parliament declared that the act was intended to address "great delays" by jailers "in making Returns to Writts of Habeas Corpus to them directed," as well as other abuses undertaken "to avoid...yielding Obedience to such Writts." By its terms, the act sought to remedy the fact that "many of the Kings [sic] Subjects have beene and

1. Blackstone once called "an Act for the better securing the Liberty of the Subject, and for Prevention of Imprisonments beyond the Seas, 1679," better known as the English Habeas Corpus Act of 1679, a "second *magna carta*."

hereafter may be long detained in Prison, in such Cases where by Law they are baylable." Toward that end, the act declared that it was "for the prevention whereof and the more speedy Releife of all persons imprisoned for any such criminall or supposed criminall Matters."

In an attempt to cõdify regular procedures for such cases, Section II of the act set forth how courts and jailers should respond upon the filing of a petition for a writ of habeas corpus. The law provided that the jailer "shall within Three dayes after the Service" of a writ "make Returne of such Writt" and bring "the Body of the Partie soe committed or restrained" before the relevant court while "certify[ing] the true causes of his Detainer or Imprisonment." Section III of the act set forth procedures for obtaining writs during the vacation periods of the courts—that is, when the courts were otherwise closed—in response to recent events, including the case of Francis Jenkes in 1676, in which vacation writs had been denied even where bail likely should have been granted. Section V of the act, building on the earlier Star Chamber Act, set forth escalating penalties to be paid to the prisoner in cases where jailers violated the obligation to make a return and produce the prisoner. Sections VI and IX curtailed the common abuses of recommitting discharged prisoners for the same offense and moving prisoners to escape a court's jurisdiction (the former being what the US Constitution refers to as "double jeopardy"). Of considerable importance, Section X made clear that judges violated the act under threat of financial penalty. Section XI clarified that the writ would run to various islands and "privileged places" within the kingdom, notwithstanding judicial precedents that previously deemed these places the equivalent of legal islands. To reach yet further abusive practices by the king and his ministers, Section XII declared that the imprisonment of any "Subject of this Realme" in Scotland, Ireland, Jersey, Guernsey, Tangier, or "Parts Garrisons Islands or Places beyond the Seas...within or without the Dominions of His Majestie" is "hereby enacted and adjudged to be illegal."

The seventh section of the act warrants special attention. That section both connected the writ of habeas corpus with the criminal process and placed specific limits on how and when the executive lawfully could detain the most serious of criminals—even alleged traitors. By its terms, the section covered "any person or persons...committed for High Treason or Fellony." Where the Crown did not indict a prisoner committed on this basis within two court terms (a period typically spanning only three to six months), the act provided that the justices of King's Bench and other criminal courts were "*required*...to sett at Liberty the Prisoner upon Baile." Underscoring the mandate, the act's seventh section declared that "if any person or persons committed as aforesaid...shall not be indicted and tryed the second Terme...or upon his Tryall shall be acquitted, he shall be discharged from his Imprisonment." Thus, the act promised that even the most dangerous of suspects who could claim the protection of domestic law—even traitors—could not be detained outside the criminal process for state reasons. Putting everything together, the habeas privilege associated with the act now curtailed the powers of the executive in new and dramatic ways, far more so than its common law ancestor had done.

But, to effectuate the act's terms, the English courts wielded the common law writ of habeas corpus as the vehicle for reviewing detentions and ultimately awarding relief where the statute required. The common law writ, Blackstone observed, also continued to serve as the vehicle for redress available in "all...cases of unjust imprisonment" that were not covered by the act, such as cases implicating liberty that fell outside the criminal context, including, for example, petitions for freedom in slavery cases. In this way, the statute and the common law writ worked together to address a spectrum of cases.

It is also in the wake of the Habeas Corpus Act's passage that the popular conception of the habeas writ as a celebrated guardian of individual liberty took flight. Thus, it was the act that Blackstone

The English origins

15

heralded in his influential *Commentaries on the Laws of England*, published between 1765 and 1769. Building on Coke's *Institutes*, Blackstone also linked the habeas privilege with the Great Charter's guarantee that one may be detained only in accordance with due process. In Blackstone's words, "*Magna carta* ... declared, that no man shall be imprisoned contrary to law: the *habeas corpus* act points him out effectual means ... to release himself." Also influential in hailing the act was Henry Care's popular treatise on *English Liberties*, first published in London in the 1680s and reprinted and widely circulated in the American colonies in the eighteenth century. Care labeled the act a "most wholesome Law" and championed it as a cure for the failings of the common law writ: "The Writ of *Habeas Corpus* is a Remedy given by the Common Law for such as were unjustly detained in Custody, to procure their Liberty: But before this Statute was rendered far less useful than it ought to be, partly by the Judges, pretending a Power to grant or deny the said Writ at their Pleasure, in many Cases; and ... [who] would oft-times alledge, That they could not take Bail, because the Party was a Prisoner of State."

Thus, at long last, Selden and Coke's aspiration to constrain the executive's power to detain outside the criminal process came to be. No longer did the king and his ministers enjoy unchecked power to detain without proceeding toward criminal trial, nor did the royal courts enjoy discretion to disregard these limitations on executive detention when ruling on habeas corpus petitions. In time, Scotland and Ireland adopted the same habeas protections in their own acts, Scotland in 1701 and Ireland in 1782.

One story highlights the potency of the new act as a constraint on the executive. Richard Creed had been arrested and imprisoned in 1660 following his participation in a movement that sought to preclude restoration of the English monarchy following the Interregnum. The Crown moved him several times, and at one point he landed at Pendennis Castle in Cornwall, which one hundred years later would house American Ethan Allen during the American Revolutionary War. When a writ of habeas corpus was dispatched to Pendennis Castle on Creed's behalf in 1669, his jailor never responded. Moved next to the island of Guernsey off the coast of Normandy, Creed remained there pursuant to a warrant that said nothing more to his jailor than he shall "keep [him] close prisoner within that our island until our further pleasure." In Creed's case, the English Habeas Corpus Act made all the difference. Some twenty years into his detention, Creed finally won his freedom when he sought a new writ under the act immediately after its passage and a court rejected the government's warrant, deeming it legally insufficient to justify his detention.

Given that members of Parliament at odds with the king promoted the English Habeas Corpus Act and drafted it with the intention of curtailing royal powers, it is curious that Charles II, the monarch restored to the throne following the English Civil War, even assented to the act at all. Whatever his motivation— historians still dispute this point—the act came at a time of considerable unrest. Specifically, many in Parliament worried over the likelihood that James—Duke of York, brother of Charles II, and a Catholic convert—would succeed to the throne on Charles's death. The unrest leading up to James II's ultimate ascension to the throne in 1685 highlighted both the limitations of the act and how much power Parliament had now claimed for itself.

Chapter 2

The limits and potential
of habeas corpus

With the Habeas Corpus Act, Parliament took control of the law of detention and established a powerful check on executive authority hand in hand with important protections of individual liberty. But the act's limitations quickly came to light. To begin, as a geographic matter, the Crown took the position that the act did not extend to the edges of the empire. Thus, following the act's passage, the practice of moving prisoners to so-called legal islands—even those specifically mentioned in the act—continued. In 1683, for example, the government arrested a number of alleged Scottish conspirators in the Rye House Plot, which aimed to assassinate Charles II and his heir to the throne, his brother James, then Duke of York. Although the prisoners had been arrested in England on suspicion of treason committed there, the Scots Privy Council, presided over by the king, ordered them dispatched to Scotland, where the Habeas Corpus Act did not apply.

In short order, two additional—and substantial—means of circumventing the act emerged. The first, parliamentary bills of attainder, declared a person or group guilty of a crime and punished them in the absence of any trial. The plight of Charles II's son, the Duke of Monmouth, reveals the potency of attainder. Monmouth, who was born out of wedlock, had been exiled from England in 1683 in the wake of the failed Rye House Plot. After the death of his father and the crowning of James II in 1685, Monmouth returned to England determined to wrestle the throne from his uncle. Once Monmouth was captured, James ordered him sent to the Tower of London. Days later, Parliament passed a bill of attainder in which it declared Monmouth summarily guilty of treason and ordered his execution. His gruesome public beheading on Tower Hill followed in due course. Meanwhile, scores of his followers were executed or sold into slavery without trial. Parliament continued to wield its potent and essentially unchecked attainder power for some time to come.

Meanwhile, the crowning of James II witnessed more unrest, exacerbated by the new Catholic king's efforts to reverse many of Parliament's anti-Catholic policies adopted during his brother's reign. After James's second wife, a Catholic, gave birth to a Catholic son and likely heir to the throne, opposition nobility formalized an invitation to William of Orange to invade. When William landed on English shores in 1688, James fled to France to seek refuge in the protection of his cousin, King Louis XIV. The crowning of William and his wife Mary, James II's daughter from his earlier Protestant marriage, marked the Glorious Revolution. Their reign witnessed the restoration of a Protestant monarchy, the continued rise of parliamentary supremacy, greater independence for the royal courts, and the adoption of the Declaration of Rights. But James II's supporters—the so-called Jacobites—began plotting almost immediately to engineer his return to the throne. To counter their efforts, Parliament created a new tool for setting aside the protections of the Habeas Corpus Act—*suspension*.

The first suspension of the English Habeas Corpus Act came only months into the reign of William and Mary in 1689 and established an important precedent for future suspensions. Parliament acted as James was plotting with French assistance to return to England to retake his throne and while Ireland was in revolt and Scotland was on the verge of the same. Through an emissary, William requested the Houses of Parliament to grant him the power to arrest suspected Jacobites and detain them without trial. William made the request, his emissary explained, because "the King is not willing to do any thing but what he may be warranted by Law; therefore, if these persons deliver themselves by *Habeas Corpus*, there may arise a difficulty." After considerable debate, both houses moved forward with suspension legislation, and the House of Lords declared that it had done so to authorize the king to "secure[ ] all such suspected Persons, as may effectually prevent any Disturbance of the Public Peace."

Parliament entitled its statute "An Act for Impowering His Majestie to Apprehend and Detaine such Persons as He shall finde just Cause to Suspect are Conspireing against the Government." By its terms, the act explicitly set aside "the Benefitt and Advantage" of the Habeas Corpus Act for those "persons" suspected of high treason who were committed by a warrant signed by six members of the Privy Council. It then displaced "all other Laws and Statutes any way" relating to the liberty of the subject, establishing the principle that suspension also set aside laws and legal practices that were complementary to the act—including the common law writ of habeas corpus. The act likewise prohibited any "Judge or other Person" from bailing or trying such prisoners. Finally, by its title the act purported to "impower" the Crown to order the arrests of those it believed were "conspiring against the government." Undoubtedly aware that it was handing the Crown a potent emergency authority—the ability to arrest and detain suspected traitors without trial—Parliament declared that this first suspension would run for only one month.

Waves of arrests followed the act's passage. Then, as its date of expiration approached and some of those detained sought their freedom while invoking their rights under the English Habeas Corpus Act, Parliament extended the suspension. In so doing, Parliament expanded the scope of those who could order arrests to include privy counselors and expanded those who could be arrested to include those suspected of so-called treasonable practices. During the debates over these early suspensions, virtually every speaker in Parliament equated suspension with freeing the executive from having to prosecute those arrested. Thus, one member of Parliament explained, "the Law of *Habeas Corpus*" ensured that "a man may know his crime before he be committed to prison" and test the sufficiency of the grounds of the charges against him during that process. Suspension, by contrast, displaced this framework and thereby empowered the Crown to arrest and detain on suspicion alone. When the extension finally lapsed, the legal framework of the Habeas Corpus Act returned immediately to effect, and it is here that one finds records of droves of prisoners being ordered discharged by the Court of King's Bench.

Accordingly, suspension marked a dramatic alteration of the law of habeas corpus, authorizing arrests on suspicion alone and sidelining the courts from being able to offer any relief to those swept up within the terms of the acts. In a debate over one of Parliament's earliest suspensions, Sir William Whitlock's remarks underscored the dramatic nature of suspension. As he phrased things, "If an Angel came from Heaven that was a Privy-Counsellor, I would not trust my Liberty with him one moment."

Additional suspensions followed in response to war with France and continuing Jacobite threats in 1696, 1708, 1715, 1722, 1744, and 1745. In each case, Parliament modeled the suspensions on the precedent of 1689, setting aside either the English Habeas Corpus Act or its Scottish equivalent, as well as all other legal protections that prisoners might claim. With each new experiment with suspension, however, Parliament became more aggressive. Thus, Parliament provided that some of the later suspensions would last up to one year in length, a fact that provoked dissent from those who feared the abuses that might follow under such authorizations.

The final suspension declared by Parliament before the American Revolution, in 1745, coincided with the landing of Charles Edward Stuart, known as both "the Young Pretender" and "Bonnie Prince Charlie," in Scotland. The Young Pretender had raised the Jacobite standard at Glenfinnan and led troops to overtake the city of Edinburgh. But in short order, the cause fell when royal troops quickly and soundly routed the Jacobites on Culloden Moor in the Scottish Highlands in April 1746. It was only after completion of the sorting of the prisoners in the wake of Culloden that Parliament allowed the suspension of 1745 to lapse.

Throughout these decades, on more than one occasion, King's Bench explained the effect of a suspension, drawing on the original 1689 precedent. Take the case of Sir William Wyndham, a leading Jacobite who had been committed to the Tower of London for high treason during the 1715 suspension. Wyndham's initial attempt to win bail from King's Bench failed, coming as it did during the suspension. When the 1715 suspension lapsed, Wyndham tried again. This time he succeeded, with King's Bench holding that in light of the passage of four terms since his commitment, "there being no prosecution against him, he must be admitted to bail." Wyndham's case confirmed that when a suspension ended, the protections of the Habeas Corpus Act immediately returned to force and the royal courts were bound to honor its mandates.

Another case, brought by several prominent prisoners in the Tower of London during the 1722 suspension, also clarified the relationship between the Habeas Corpus Act and suspension. The so-called Prisoners in the Tower, who were alleged to be conspiring to restore the Stuart line on the throne, argued that they should win their freedom because the jurisdiction of the Court of King's Bench "is invested with an ordinary and extraordinary power, which cannot be taken away by implication in any statute." The court rejected the argument while confirming that any power it enjoyed by reason of the Habeas Corpus Act,

2. Royal troops battle Scottish Highlanders, who supported the Jacobite cause, in 1745. One year later, the cause would expire on Culloden Moor, bringing to an end the movement to restore the Stuart line to the British throne.

along with any other discretion it might otherwise possess to grant relief to the prisoners—including any common law power—had been displaced by the act of suspension. This important decision established that even the jurisdiction of the great King's Bench and the majestic writ of habeas corpus existed at the mercy of Parliament.

Finally, in several cases involving the rebels who had fought with the Young Pretender to reinstate the Stuart line, the Court of King's Bench rejected the legal defense that they had renounced their allegiance to the king and sworn fidelity to Charles. When the chief justice, Sir William Lee, pronounced the judgments following the London trials of one group of rebels, he chastised the defendants for "falsely pretending that they were entitled to the same Treatment as the Subjects of a Foreign Prince taken Prisoners of war." Instead, he declared, they were guilty of treason. As this and other cases during the period highlight, those deemed to owe allegiance bore an obligation of loyalty to the Crown. Although this rendered such persons vulnerable to prosecution for treason, it also meant that such persons could claim the protections of domestic law, including, where applicable, the Habeas Corpus Act.

By contrast, those captured in war who were in the service of a foreign enemy and who did not owe allegiance were treated as prisoners of war and left to claim any legal protections from the law of nations. Thus, as Blackstone wrote in the eighteenth century, borrowing from Coke and Sir Matthew Hale (who had served as chief justice of King's Bench during the early years of the Habeas Corpus Act), "alien-enemies have no rights, no privileges, unless by the king's special favour, during the time of war." Putting all of this together, during this period, the ability to invoke the Habeas Corpus Act—and the need to suspend the same to hold persons outside the criminal process—was linked inextricably to the bond of allegiance as that term was then understood.

In the lead-up to the American Revolution, English law witnessed many important developments that would come to influence Anglo-American law for generations. Further, it is during this period that the writ of habeas corpus became a writ of liberty. Along the way, events also underscored the continuing relevance of the common law writ of habeas corpus.

On the heels of the English Habeas Corpus Act, in 1689, Parliament adopted the English Bill of Rights. As an initial matter, the Bill of Rights defended James II's ouster from the throne and resolved that William and Mary were the rightful king and queen of England. Next, the bill asserted parliamentary supremacy. It then proclaimed that the people enjoyed a series of rights, while at the same time set forth limitations on the power of the Crown. Thus, for example, the Bill of Rights declared that the Crown was powerless to suspend or dispense with the law, to levy money without parliamentary assent, and to raise an army in peacetime. The Bill of Rights also declared that members of Parliament enjoyed the rights to free speech and free election and that the people enjoyed the right to petition the king for their grievances, along with protection against excessive bail, fines, and cruel and unusual punishment. In 1696, Parliament passed the Trial of Treasons Act, which instituted procedural protections for those charged with the crime of high treason. These protections included the requirement that two witnesses testify to an overt act of treason, a condition later imported into the US Constitution's treason clause. The act likewise included other protections that had not previously been granted to those accused of common law crimes, including the right to counsel and to compel witnesses for one's defense.

Viewing all of these developments together, it was no stretch for Henry Care's popular treatise on English law to point to, among other things, Magna Carta, the Habeas Corpus Act, and these additional developments collectively as the guardians of English liberties. The story of habeas corpus, once wrapped up in the power struggles between Parliament and the Crown, now became a story about liberty.

This was also true with respect to the common law writ of habeas corpus, which remained an important means by which the judiciary could remedy unlawful detention beyond those cases encompassed within the Habeas Corpus Act. No case underscores the continuing significance of the common law writ during this period better than *Somerset v. Stewart*, also known as Somerset's case (with his name sometimes spelled differently), initially heard by the Court of King's Bench during Easter term, 1772.

James Somerset had been held as a slave to an American named Charles Stewart, who brought Somerset with him to England. After Somerset ran away in 1771, he was captured and placed in the custody of a ship captain's vessel for transportation to Jamaica. There, he was set to be sold as a slave. Abolitionists, supported by Granville Sharp, England's "first abolitionist," sought a writ of habeas corpus on Somerset's behalf from King's Bench. Forced to confront the complex legal framework surrounding slavery in England and the colonies, the great chief justice of that court, Lord Mansfield, initially held the case over, suggesting that it would be better if Parliament resolved the thorny questions at the heart of the case. (As Mansfield wrote, that would be the "best, and perhaps the only method of settling the point for the future.") When Parliament did not act and King's Bench had to revisit the case some months later, Mansfield asked whether the captain's return was sufficient to justify his custody over Somerset. In confronting the question, Mansfield began by opining that the "state of slavery . . . [is] so odious, that nothing can be suffered to support it, but positive law." Finding no evidence of "approv[al]" by the law of England," he ordered Somerset's discharge and effectively granted him his freedom.

Technically, Somerset's case spoke only to the legality of the removal of a slave from the kingdom. But the decision was widely understood by courts in, among other places, Scotland and the United States as standing for the proposition that without the imprimatur of specific legislation or constitutional sanction, slavery was illegal—a proposition that these courts adopted as their own in reliance on the decision. Further, events following Somerset's case lend strong support to the conclusion that it should be read as having provided for the de jure—or legal—end of slavery in England, even though it was not until the Slave Trade Act of 1807 that Britain formally ended its involvement in the slave trade and the Slavery Abolition Act of 1833 that Britain abolished slavery in most colonies. Somerset's case therefore stands as an example of just how powerful the common law writ of habeas corpus could be, not only in protecting—but also expanding—liberty. This, too, is part of the story of the "Great Writ."

Chapter 3
Revolution

Across the Atlantic, Americans widely studied Henry Care's treatise and Blackstone's *Commentaries*, both of which glorified as the foundation of English law and liberties Magna Carta, the Petition of Right, and the Habeas Corpus Act. For his part, Blackstone, the prominent Oxford professor who eventually would sit as a justice on the Court of King's Bench, celebrated the promise of the English Habeas Corpus Act that "no man is to be arrested, unless charged with such a crime, as will at least justify holding him to bail, when taken." He also instructed that the Habeas Corpus Act had made "the remedy...now complete for *removing* the injury of unjust and illegal confinement." As Blackstone wrote, no longer could a person be "apprehended upon suspicion" alone anywhere that the act remained in force. Care and Blackstone's work was the dominant resource to which Americans turned in studying English law, and the authors' emphasis on the Habeas Corpus Act influenced strongly how Americans thought about habeas corpus.

But the American experience did not know many of the rights and protections that Care and Blackstone venerated in their writings. This was true despite the fact that from the beginning of English settlement in North America, the colonists had claimed to possess "all the rights, liberties and immunities of free and natural-born subjects, within the realm of England." In the period leading up to the Revolutionary War, the Crown repeatedly made clear that American colonists did not enjoy the same rights as their English counterparts across the Atlantic. For example, American colonists witnessed the Crown wield general warrants and writs of assistance even though general warrants had been deemed illegal in England.

Further, attempts by several colonies to adopt or invoke the protections of the Habeas Corpus Act as their own routinely failed. New York, for example, witnessed James II veto its efforts to adopt the act in 1685. He did so on the stated basis that "this Priviledge is not granted to any of His Ma^ts Plantations where the Act of Habeas Corpus and all such other Bills do not take Place." Ten years later, a similar effort by Massachusetts also met with Privy Council veto. In 1749, when the North Carolina General Assembly adopted the English Habeas Corpus Act, the king declared the colony's legislation "void and of no[] effect."

It also did not help matters in the lead-up to the Revolutionary War that in 1774 the British government rejected extending the benefit of the Habeas Corpus Act to the province of Quebec. If anything, this only fueled the American colonists' belief that they were the subjects of a tyrannical government. Anger ran so deep with respect to the events in Quebec that they bore mention in the American Declaration of Independence. (In 1784, Quebec finally secured habeas legislation, including many of the Habeas Corpus Act's terms, only to witness its suspension soon thereafter.)

Over time, the denial of the protections of the Habeas Corpus Act to the colonists became a major source of complaint regarding British rule. Thus, the American Continental Congress wrote to the people of Great Britain in 1774 to decry the fact that the colonists were "the subjects of an arbitrary government, deprived of trial by jury, and when imprisoned cannot claim the benefit of the habeas corpus Act, that great bulwark and palladium of English liberty." That same year, while soliciting Canadian support for the cause of independence, the Continental Congress declared the right to be governed by representatives of the people's choosing, the right to trial by jury, and the privilege of habeas corpus to be among the most fundamental rights. "These are the rights, without which a people cannot be free and happy."

By 1775, when British troops met local colonial militia at Lexington and Concord and then Bunker Hill, war was inevitable. In short order, the colonists formed the Continental Army and royal officials took flight from America. With war came prisoners, along with a host of legal questions as to when and how they may be detained. As things unfolded, the patchwork legal framework of the English Habeas Corpus Act—it applied in some geographic areas of the British Empire, but not in others—came to play a major role in how the British treated American prisoners captured during the Revolutionary War.

The British, however, were consistent on one key point—namely, that the American "Rebels" were traitors and therefore not in the service of a foreign sovereign. King George III declared that the colonists "forget the Allegiance which they owe to the Power that has protected and sustained them...[and] have at length proceeded to an open and avowed Rebellion, by...traitorously preparing, ordering and levying War against us." Early in the war, the capture of an important prisoner would test this idea. His name was Ethan Allen.

In 1775, following the battles at Lexington and Concord, Allen successfully led his "Green Mountain Boys" in the capture of the strategically important British stronghold at Fort Ticonderoga in upstate New York. But when he moved north, his successes ended. The British captured Allen and his "Boys" during their failed attempt to take the city of Montreal. In short order, British Lieutenant Governor Cramahé ordered Allen, along with his cohort of "Rebel Prisoners," dispatched to England. Cramahé did so, in his words, because he had "no proper Place to confine them in, or Troops to guard Them," in Canada. After a weeks-long journey across the Atlantic, the prisoners landed in Falmouth, England, days before Christmas in 1775. The British imprisoned Allen and his Boys at Pendennis Castle in Cornwall, where Richard Creed had been detained a century earlier. But within only a few days, the British legal elite met and decided to send Allen and his fellow Rebels back to America as soon as possible. Why?

The answer speaks volumes about how habeas law during this period was tied inextricably to geography and notions of allegiance. Initially, political calculations appear to have influenced the decision, stemming from the North administration's apparent uncertainty as to whether it could successfully prosecute the Rebels as traitors in light of the existence of some sympathy for their plight. Upon hearing that Allen had been reportedly "thrown into irons and suffers all the hardships inflicted upon common felons," General George Washington had also threatened retaliation against a British prisoner, the British general Richard Prescott. But also likely important was the fact that efforts apparently were underway to invoke the protections of the English Habeas Corpus Act in the British courts on behalf of Allen and his fellow Rebels. Internal documents memorializing British officials debating what to do with Allen make reference to these efforts and suggest that they significantly influenced events. As one admiralty lord wrote just days after Allen's arrival in England, the administration's "principal object" must be "to get the prisoners out of reach as soon as possible." Out of reach of what?

The answer, most likely, was the British courts. There, someone like Allen—a person who could claim British subjecthood and who was held on English soil—had the right to invoke the protections of the English Habeas Corpus Act and thereby force his trial or else secure his freedom. But across the Atlantic, the Habeas Corpus Act did not apply—or at least, that was the position that the Crown had taken for some time. Thus, by sending Allen back across the Atlantic, the administration could elude the Habeas Corpus Act. And that is precisely what the administration did. (Notably, Allen wrote in his *Narrative* that while on his journey back to America, his irons were removed and "this remove was in consequence, as I have been since informed, of a writ of habeas corpus, which had been procured by some gentlemen in England, in order to obtain me my liberty.")

As the Revolutionary War continued, British ships began arriving in a constant stream to deposit American prisoners on British shores, forcing the administration to confront head-on the legal status of American Rebels held on English soil, where the Habeas Corpus Act was in full effect. To sort out its options, the administration consulted Lord Mansfield, seeking his advice regarding how to treat a specific group of American officers captured on the high seas. In Mansfield's view, the prisoners were "guilty of high treason in levying war." This, however, presented various "difficult[ies]." Mansfield advised that if the Americans "were prisoners of war the King might keep them where he pleased; consequently aboard a guardship no *habeas corpus* could deliver them." But, he continued, "if [the American prisoners] are so wickedly advised as to claim to be considered as subjects and apply for a *habeas corpus*, it is their own doing; they force a regular commitment for their crime." In other words, Mansfield believed that the only way to keep them in detention would be if the "Attorney-General upon information of their crime properly sworn" presented it "as a ground for their commitment." This confirmed what the administration already believed—namely, that in England, the Habeas Corpus Act prohibited the detention of American Rebels outside the criminal process.

Accordingly, in early 1777, Prime Minister Frederick North turned to the same tool that had been wielded during earlier periods of unrest—suspension. Introducing a suspension bill to Parliament, North explained that in times of "rebellion, or danger of invasion," it had been customary "to enable the king to seize suspected persons." But, he continued, "as the law stood," this was not possible. Accordingly, he pleaded, "it was necessary for the crown to have a power of confining them like other prisoners of war." Parliament responded with what came to be known as North's Act.

As enacted, the suspension legislation applied only to persons suspected of high treason or piracy committed in America or on the high seas, and it authorized their detention without bail or release upon surety. Parliament was careful to target only Americans and did so for the purpose of addressing "a Rebellion and War [that] ha[s] been openly and traiterously levied and carried on in certain of his Majesty's Colonies and Plantations in *America*, and Acts of Treason and Piracy [that] have been committed on the High Seas." As the act explained, a suspension was necessary because "it may be inconvenient in many such Cases to proceed forthwith to the Trial of such Criminals, and at the same Time of evil Example to suffer them to go at large." Parliament subsequently extended the legislation several times to last through much of the war.

In response to North's Act, George Washington complained in his *Manifesto* that Parliament had now sanctioned "arbitrary imprisonment" by reason of the "suspension of the Habeas Corpus Act." In this respect, the act further fueled the American belief that they were the subjects of a tyrannical government.

Over the course of the Revolutionary War, the act rendered lawful the indefinite detention without trial of almost three thousand captured Americans brought to England for imprisonment, many of whom were committed to Mill and Forton Prisons, while a handful were committed to Edinburgh Castle and various London prisons. Those imprisoned in London included the American painter (and former aide to General Washington) John Trumbull as well as the former president of the Continental Congress Henry Laurens, who was dispatched to the Tower of London. Laurens's

LIBERTY SUSPENDED! with the Bulwark of the Constitution!

3. "Liberty suspended! With the Bulwark of the Constitution!" A satirical print by George Cruikshank condemns a British suspension of habeas corpus in 1817. A printing press serves as a scaffold, from which Liberty hangs, gagged, bound, and holding a scroll inscribed with the watchwords of British constitutionalism, "Magna Charta, Bill of Rights, Habeas Corpus." From the platform, the Leader of the House of Commons, Lord Castlereagh, defends the suspension, victoriously holding aloft Liberty's broken staff.

story reveals the different views that the Americans and British took of one another. Laurens had been captured on the high seas en route to secure the support of the Netherlands for American independence. When taken to London, he claimed to be an ambassador and argued, accordingly, that imprisoning him violated the Law of Nations. This married with the American view that the United States was an independent nation; it also conformed with the American treatment of captured British soldiers as prisoners of war.

The British, however, viewed Laurens not as an ambassador in the service of a foreign sovereign, but as a traitor promoting an unlawful rebellion. He was therefore committed to the tower on a charge of high treason. Laurens did not win his freedom until some fifteen months later as part of a prisoner exchange for Lord Cornwallis, whose surrender at Yorktown had turned the tide of the war decisively against the British. (Notably, Cornwallis was formally constable of the Tower of London where Laurens had been detained.) But Laurens was not freed from the tower outright. To the contrary, he secured his freedom only upon posting a bond and agreeing to return to appear at Easter term of the Court of King's Bench to defend himself against treason charges at trial.

During the suspension, which ran through much of the war, King's Bench once again had the chance to opine on the application of the Habeas Corpus Act. And, just as it had in the case of the prisoners in the tower in 1722, the court reaffirmed that the act— and, with it, all of its protections—was displaced by a suspension. King's Bench did so in the case of an American named Ebenezer Platt, who had been involved in the first capture of a British ship in the colonies and captured some time later by the British in Jamaica before being transported to English shores. Announcing the court's decision respecting Platt's habeas petition during Easter term 1777, Lord Mansfield proclaimed that "the purpose of the [suspension] Act is to prevent the Necessity of the Trial." This, he declared, meant that the Americans in custody on English soil under North's Act, including Platt, had no legal recourse to win their freedom.

It was only once independence became a foregone conclusion in 1782 that Parliament finally permitted the oft-extended suspension to lapse. In its place, Parliament adopted a provision declaring that the British government's relationship with the American prisoners—now viewed as being in the service of a newly acknowledged (if not yet formally recognized) independent country—would no longer be governed by domestic law. Instead, the Americans now could be discharged or exchanged "according to the Custom and Usage of War, and the Law of Nations," the international legal framework that governed relations between nations. Under this regime, by March 1783 the British delivered all American prisoners remaining in England to France.

The United States of America now had a country, and a legal framework, to build. And so they set to work.

Chapter 4
Habeas corpus comes to America

In the newly formed United States, the principles of the English Habeas Corpus Act finally took root. Surveying this period, one finds pervasive evidence that the act and its protections wielded profound influence over the development of early American habeas jurisprudence. Meanwhile, American law also imported a robust common law writ of habeas corpus that would fulfill many of the same roles in American law as it had in English law and reach cases beyond the scope of the English act. But it is the Habeas Corpus Act that was at the center of developments leading up to ratification of a habeas clause in the US Constitution.

Until independence, the American colonial experience of numerous failed attempts to adopt the English Habeas Corpus Act bore considerable resemblance to the Irish experience. That country had witnessed seventeen failed attempts by the Irish House of Commons over the course of some ninety years to adopt the English act before the Privy Council finally approved an Irish act in 1782. It took a war for independence for Americans to secure those same protections.

During the American Revolution and the years that followed, a wave of states adopted (or, in some cases, reaffirmed) the core terms of the English Habeas Corpus Act—including particularly its seventh section. Some states did so by writing the act's protections into their constitutions, others by enacting statutes, and still others through common law decisions handed down by their courts.

As one of its first acts as an independent government, for example, South Carolina's General Assembly in March 1776 adopted an "Ordinance to vest the several Powers...formerly granted to the Council of Safety in the President and Privy Council to suspend the Habeas Corpus Act." A few decades later, South Carolina formally adopted the English act verbatim as part of its code. And in its Constitution of 1777, Georgia provided that "the principles of the Habeas Corpus Act, shall be part of this Constitution." (To be all the more clear as to what those principles were, the Georgia legislature annexed verbatim copies of the English Habeas Corpus Act to the Georgia Constitution's original distribution.) The Massachusetts Constitution of 1780, in turn, expressly connected the habeas privilege to the concept of suspension. Together, these developments underscore the influence of the act and the English suspension model more generally.

During the Revolutionary War, moreover, at least six of the newly declared independent states enacted their own suspension acts modeled on the English precedents from the late seventeenth and eighteenth centuries to legalize the detention of the disaffected outside the criminal process. Notably, some of these suspensions expressly set aside the Habeas Corpus Act. For example, in Maryland, suspension legislation enacted during the war declared that "during any invasion of this state by the enemy, the *habeas corpus* act shall be suspended, as to all such persons."

And just three months before the Constitutional Convention convened in Philadelphia during the fateful year of 1787, New York passed a statute almost identical to the English Habeas Corpus Act. The legislation, which tracked the seventh section of its English predecessor, made explicit the requirement that any person "committed for any treason or felony" who is not "indicted and tried [by] the second term [of the] sessions" of the relevant court "after his commitment...shall be discharged from his imprisonment." Highlighting the pervasive influence of the English Habeas Corpus Act on the development of early American law, the great New York jurist and legal commentator Chancellor James Kent observed in 1827 that "the statute of 31 Charles II. c. 2 [the English Habeas Corpus Act]...is the basis of all the American statutes on the subject."

Such was the backdrop against which the delegates convened in Philadelphia to draft a new constitution and replace the short-lived Articles of Confederation that initially governed the newly independent country. As they set to work, the convention delegates established a government framework that provided for the strict separation of powers among legislative, executive, and judicial branches. As they turned to the judiciary, they mandated the creation of a national Supreme Court and authorized Congress, at its discretion, to establish inferior federal courts. The delegates also included a habeas clause, known as the Suspension Clause. Initially, the habeas clause resided in the judiciary article alongside the clause guaranteeing that "the trial of all crimes (except in cases of impeachment) shall be by jury." It is easy to see why the two concepts started out as neighbors in the draft, given the close connection that had long existed between the protections of the English Habeas Corpus Act and the guarantee of a criminal trial.

The original proposal for a habeas clause came just four days after the convention came to order, when Charles Pinckney introduced a draft plan for a constitution that included a provision prohibiting suspension "except in case of rebellion or invasion." Where he derived this phrase is unclear, but one possible source is the Irish Habeas Corpus Act, which had been adopted five years earlier. In their act, the Irish imported much of the language of the 1679 English act verbatim, with the notable addition of a provision empowering, while also constraining, the Irish Council to suspend the act "during such time only as there shall be an actual invasion or rebellion in this kingdom or Great Britain."

In all events, some months later and after limited debate, the delegates embraced language introduced by Pennsylvania delegate Gouverneur Morris, which read, "The privilege of the writ of Habeas Corpus shall not be suspended, unless where in cases of Rebellion or invasion the public safety may require it." Notably, Morris's cousin, Isaac Gouverneur, had been detained in England under the suspension that governed during the American Revolution. One could surmise that as a result, Morris powerfully appreciated the dramatic nature of suspension. In all events, as debate on Morris's proposal ensued, some states objected to recognition of any suspension power in the Constitution. But they were outnumbered. At this point, the language went to the Committee of Style, on which Morris served. As it made final edits on the draft Constitution, the committee modified the Suspension Clause by substituting "when" for "where." Likewise, it moved the clause to the Constitution's first article, which set forth the parameters of the legislative branch, placing the clause alongside the prohibition on bills of attainder. Here, too, there was synergy between the clauses, given that like suspension, bills of attainder had been wielded by the British Parliament at the expense of individual liberty.

Once the delegates had completed their work, the Constitution went to the states for consideration. During the state ratifying conventions and debates that took place in the wake of the Philadelphia convention, speaker after speaker connected the Suspension Clause with the English Habeas Corpus Act and, more generally, the criminal process. Thus, for example, in promoting the draft Constitution in *The Federalist*, Alexander Hamilton lauded the fact that the document provided for "trial by jury in criminal cases, aided by the *habeas corpus act*." For his part, in objecting to the portion of the habeas clause that implicitly authorized suspension, Luther Martin of Maryland described the clause as permitting the suspension of "the Act of Ha: Corpus." Another critic of the draft Constitution, the Anti-Federalist publication the *Federal Farmer*, took issue with the document's omission of a bill of rights, but nonetheless pointed to the Suspension Clause and its neighboring provisions as "a partial bill of rights" and celebrated the fact that the Constitution "recognize[d] or re-establish[ed] the benefits [of] that writ, and the jury trial in criminal cases." Thus, the *Federal Farmer* explained, "The people by adopting the federal constitution" ensured that "the benefits of the habeas corpus act shall be enjoyed by individuals." Numerous similar statements made by speakers throughout the state ratification debates abound connecting the Suspension Clause with the English Habeas Corpus Act. Highlighting the strong connection between the English Habeas Corpus Act and the clause, Chief Justice Marshall would write a few decades later that when interpreting the latter, one must look to "that law which is in a considerable degree incorporated into our own"—specifically, "the celebrated *habeas corpus* act" of 1679.

In the same ratification debates, many, including Luther Martin, raised concerns that the suspension authority could prove a potent vehicle for oppression and abuse. Others questioned whether the clause's implicit recognition of such a power underscored the need for a bill of rights given the lack of an affirmative grant of such a power in the constitutional text. Indeed, this proved important fodder for the argument of Anti-Federalists that there existed the possibility that other sweeping powers not expressly granted to the government might similarly be invoked at the expense of individual rights. In time, these concerns would drive ratification of the first ten amendments to the Constitution, the Bill of Rights. Writing in *The Federalist*, Hamilton cited the draft Suspension Clause to argue that was unnecessary: "Arbitrary impeachments, arbitrary methods of prosecuting pretended offenses, and arbitrary punishments upon arbitrary convictions have ever appeared to me to be the great engines of judicial despotism; and these have all relation to criminal proceedings. The trial by jury in criminal cases, aided by the *habeas corpus* act, seems therefore to be alone concerned in the question. And both of these are provided for in the most ample manner in the plan of the convention."

Given all that the Habeas Corpus Act and its protections had long been understood to embody and guarantee when coupled with the jury trial right—among other things, the right to presentment or indictment, the right to a speedy trial by one's peers, and a prohibition on double jeopardy—Hamilton's contention that an express Bill of Rights was unnecessary for the protection of individual liberty had some force.

All the same, a Bill of Rights did follow immediately on the heels of ratification of the Constitution in 1791. Among its ten amendments, the fifth included a due process clause providing that "No person shall be ... deprived of life, liberty, or property, without due process of law." Built upon the foundation established in Chapter 39 of Magna Carta, the US Constitution now likewise promised that no one could be deprived of liberty except in conformity with the law of the land. This, too, would prove important to the story of the writ of habeas corpus.

As the ratification debates over the Suspension Clause unfolded, some participants argued that the judiciary would protect against any abuse of the suspension authority. For example, Chief Justice William Cushing of the Massachusetts Supreme Judicial Court opined that "the clause appears to me so plain, that if a Judge should refuse a citizen his hab. Corps., after a rebellion was over, or the invasion at an end; I think *he* ought to be impeached & degraded from his office." Cushing therefore believed that judges were obliged to recognize the privilege at all times in the absence of a proper suspension, a position echoed in St. George Tucker's important early treatise on American law.

Others were not so sure. Although he would soon draft the Bill of Rights, during the ratification debates, James Madison wrote to his friend and fellow Virginian Thomas Jefferson that he doubted how well "written prohibitions" on the suspension authority would hold up. As he put it, "Should a Rebellion or insurrection alarm the people as well as the Govt, and a suspension of the Hab Corp be dictated by the alarm, no written prohibitions on earth would prevent the measure." Time would reveal that Madison, in comparison to Chief Justice Cushing, was a better predictor of human tendencies.

Chapter 5
Habeas corpus in the early United States

When the First US Congress met after the 1789 ratification of the Constitution, it had a lot of work to do. Training its attention on establishing a federal court system, Congress passed the Judiciary Act of 1789. The act did many things, including establish inferior, or lower, federal courts that sit below the Supreme Court of the United States. Section 14 of the act also vested habeas jurisdiction in the federal courts. Two decades later, Chief Justice John Marshall wrote in Ex parte *Bollman* that "the power to award the writ by any of the courts of the United States...must be given by written law." Nonetheless, he observed that the First Congress, "acting under the immediate influence of th[e] [Suspension Clause], must have felt, with peculiar force, the obligation of providing efficient means by which this great constitutional privilege should receive life and activity; for if the means not be in existence, the privilege itself would be lost, although no law for its suspension should be enacted." Ever since *Bollman*, scholars have debated what Marshall meant by referring to an "obligation." Does it spring from the Constitution itself? (Recall, Marshall also placed considerable emphasis on "written law.") The question is largely academic, because with the exception of a handful of situations—namely, two federal suspensions during and following the Civil War and legislation enacted in the wake of the terrorist attacks of September 11, 2001—Section 14's provision for general habeas jurisdiction has remained a constant throughout American history. It is through Section 14's grant—still in existence in the twenty-first century in the US code as 28 U.S.C. § 2241—as well as the robust common law tradition derived from English law, that the writ of habeas corpus has remained a crucial instrument by which American judges have checked executive abuses and protected individual liberty.

Meanwhile, suspension has been a rare occurrence in US history. In the early years of the Republic, president after president declined to request acts of suspension when faced with domestic insurrections and war. This was true, for example, with respect to the Whiskey Rebellion, an uprising of farmers and distillers in Pennsylvania who protested a federal whiskey tax. In response, the first president, George Washington, called forth the militia because the insurgents had proven "too powerful to be suppressed by the ordinary course of judicial proceedings or by the power vested in the [United States] marshals." In so doing, Washington never considered a suspension; instead, he ordered his general, Henry Lee, to "deliver" the leaders of the rebellion "to the civil magistrates" to be evaluated for criminal prosecution. Washington's successor, John Adams, followed a similar course during his presidency in suppressing Fries's Rebellion, another Pennsylvania-based rebellion over taxes.

Even the return of war between British and American forces on American soil in 1812 did not witness the fourth US president, James Madison, suspend the privilege. (Then–Major General Andrew Jackson, however, did declare a suspension in New Orleans during the war, all on his own.) In keeping with the model established during Washington's presidency, the Madison administration and the courts subscribed to the position that citizens suspected of aiding the British during the war could not be detained in the absence of criminal charges. (Madison and the courts also adhered to the position that such persons could not be tried by military tribunals.) It did not matter that the First Congress had defined a traitor as "any person . . . owing allegiance to the United States of America [who] shall levy war against them, or shall adhere to their enemies." Those owing allegiance, whether suspected traitors or not, enjoyed full rights under domestic law.

Between these events, however, the third president of the United States, Thomas Jefferson, initially charted a different course. In 1807, Jefferson promoted a suspension in response to the so-called Burr conspiracy. Aaron Burr, Jefferson's vice president during his first term, had set out to explore the Western territories, spearheading—according to Jefferson—"an illegal combination of private individuals against the peace and safety of the Union." (Allegedly, Burr sought to form an independent country out of portions of the United States and Mexico. How far any such efforts went remains disputed to this day.) Jefferson's support for a suspension marked a departure from his ratification-era views, which questioned the recognition of any suspension power, fearing its abuse at the hands of the executive.

Jefferson lamented to Congress that one of the "principal emissaries of Mr. Burr ... had been liberated by *habeas corpus*" and likewise complained that a "premature attempt to bring Burr to justice" in Kentucky had failed "without sufficient evidence for his conviction." In these statements, Jefferson recognized that detaining key actors in the conspiracy might not be possible in conformity with the ordinary criminal process; this explains why through an emissary he sought a suspension.

The day after Jefferson's remarks, the Senate took up the first proposed federal suspension legislation with the objective of legalizing the detention of alleged Burr conspirators without charges. The measure quickly passed in the Senate before running into opposition in the House. House opponents stressed that prosecution in the ordinary course would be sufficient to address the alleged conspiracy, which consisted of nothing more than "a few desperadoes," according to John W. Eppes, a Virginia representative and Jefferson's son-in-law. Many also echoed the sentiments of Virginian William Burwell, who posited that "nothing but the most imperious necessity would excuse us in confining to the Executive, or any person under him, the power of seizing and confining a citizen, upon bare suspicion, for three months, without responsibility, for the abuse of such unlimited discretion." Recognizing the extraordinary emergency power that suspension constituted, the House members voted overwhelmingly, 113–19, to defeat the measure.

Jefferson's administration wasted little time in regrouping and filed criminal charges against two alleged Burr conspirators who were currently in military custody and had been detained without proper warrants. In so doing, the administration was no doubt aware of the Supreme Court's decision just one year earlier in the 1806 case of John Atkins Burford, whom the government had detained as "an evil doer and disturber of the peace" without any formal charges. When Burford challenged the legality of his detention, the court held that a warrant that fails to state a criminal offense is "illegal" and requires a court to discharge a prisoner. All the same, when the government eventually did file charges in the case of the two alleged Burr conspirators who had been transferred from military custody, the high court still ordered their release in habeas after it concluded that the government had presented insufficient evidence to sustain the treason charges leveled against them.

This episode reveals several important lessons about the privilege and suspension in the early American legal tradition. First, there existed a working assumption by both Congress and President Jefferson that it was for Congress to determine whether circumstances warranted a suspension, for Jefferson pivoted to file criminal charges against the conspirators once the proposed suspension failed in the House. Second, all three branches of government agreed that suspension was a necessary predicate for detaining persons owing allegiance outside the criminal process.

Finally, John Marshall's Supreme Court viewed its role in habeas cases as robust and very much derived from English legal tradition.

In keeping with this idea, American judges more generally understood their role in habeas cases as derived from English tradition. This proved true in many contexts, including with respect to the contested issue of slavery that ultimately led to the Civil War. It was to free runaway, or so-called fugitive, slaves, that the writ enjoyed one of its finest hours.

The US Congress passed the first Fugitive Slave Act in 1793 to enforce the Constitution's Fugitive Slave Clause. The act provided that a person claiming ownership of a "fugitive from labor" could seize the individual and seek a warrant in federal court granting permission to return with the escaped slave to one's home state. The act also provided that penalties should be levied against those who obstructed its operation. Many Northern abolitionist states sought to frustrate the act by enacting "personal liberty" laws, some of which guaranteed fugitive slaves the right to seek habeas corpus relief in state courts. (Some states also adopted antikidnaping laws targeting those who captured fugitive slaves.) Judges in these states viewed their authority in habeas corpus proceedings as vast. They would often study the complete record in fugitive slave cases to give petitioners broader opportunities to make a claim for freedom. Many of these courts, moreover, relied on Lord Mansfield's opinion in *Somerset v. Stewart* as support for a robust habeas writ in this context.

During this period, free Blacks also turned to the writ for their protection. Take the case of Ralph Gould. Born free in Boston, Massachusetts, Gould had served in the US Navy. In 1839, a Washington, DC, constable arrested him and committed him to prison as a runaway slave. Facing being sold into slavery, Gould petitioned Chief Judge William Cranch of the US Circuit Court for the District of Columbia for a writ of habeas corpus. After he

W. 1839. June 11. | Runaway discharged

Ralph Gold

Hob: Carpus

Being satisfied by Evidence that the within named Ralph Gould, who was committed as a Runaway slave is not such, but is a freeman I have ordered him to be discharged.

W. Cranch

June 11 . 1839

4. Chief Judge William Cranch of the Circuit Court for the District of Columbia orders the release of Ralph Gould, a freeman who had been falsely arrested and imprisoned as a runaway slave in 1839.

presented the judge with evidence that he was a freeman, surviving papers show that Cranch ordered him discharged. As Gould's case and those of so many others seeking to win, or simply preserve, their freedom in the lead-up to the Civil War demonstrate, habeas corpus played a critical role in securing the freedom of all persons.

But such actions met resistance in Washington. Congress reinforced the original Fugitive Slave Act by passing the Force Act of 1833 and a second Fugitive Slave Act in 1850. (The latter formed part of the Compromise of 1850, a package of laws passed by Congress that made a series of compromises on the issue of slavery with respect to the slave trade and the existence of slavery in new territories, an attempt to ward off the Union breaking apart over the issue.) The 1850 act provided for expedited proceedings for returning fugitive slaves to the states from which they had fled. Northern resistance remained substantial. Indeed, after the 1850 act, many abolitionist states in the North enacted new habeas statutes specifically designed to help people who had been captured as fugitive slaves. These statutes also often empowered state courts to question the constitutionality of the federal fugitive slave laws. In one notable case, *Ableman v. Booth*, the Wisconsin Supreme Court twice granted habeas relief to Sherman Booth, who had been arrested and then prosecuted for violating the 1850 act when he helped a runaway slave escape from jail. In an 1859 opinion written by Chief Justice Roger B. Taney, the Supreme Court held that the state court was powerless to order federal officers to release Booth, thereby cutting off this avenue of resistance.

Nonetheless, the resistance of Northern states and their courts to fugitive slave laws reveals the potential for habeas corpus to serve as a great champion of liberty. The fugitive slave habeas cases also helped pave the way for a different future. Although Congress did not repeal the fugitive slave laws until well into the Civil War (specifically, in 1864), Congress came to appreciate the ability of the writ to protect former slaves and their newfound freedoms and rights granted by the Constitution soon thereafter. To this end, during the Reconstruction period following the war, Congress enacted habeas legislation in 1867 that expanded the power of federal courts to uphold federal rights and grant release to persons—including former slaves—unlawfully detained by recalcitrant states. The federal courts, once employed to foil freedom, now became a beacon for it.

But before Reconstruction, a "clear, flagrant, and gigantic case of Rebellion"—to borrow President Lincoln's words—tore apart the Union. As will be seen, many long-settled propositions with respect to the role of habeas corpus and suspension would come to be questioned during this critical period in American history.

Chapter 6
Civil war and suspension

With the Confederate attack on Fort Sumter on April 12, 1861, a bloody civil war began. President Lincoln viewed the secession of the Confederate states as illegal and considered those who supported the Confederacy traitors who owed allegiance to the Union. In this regard, his view of the secessionists mirrored that held by the British of the American Rebels decades earlier. As the war came, Lincoln acted quickly—and controversially—to protect critical areas by claiming the unilateral power to suspend habeas and delegating the power to his military generals. Under this framework, the military wielded suspension as a tool for detaining both Confederate soldiers and those who supported the cause outside the criminal process.

Lincoln proclaimed these early suspensions unilaterally and without congressional approval. To be sure, initially Congress was unable to meet to grant him this authority, but well after the body reconvened and for the next two years while it debated passing suspension legislation, Lincoln kept right on declaring suspensions on his own. His proclamations culminated in two issued in August and September of 1862 that effectively covered anyone arrested for disloyal practices and/or detained by military authorities—in other words, any and all prisoners taken into custody by the Union during the war.

5. President Abraham Lincoln suspended habeas corpus numerous times before Congress did so in 1863. He later claimed that his actions were "indispensable to the preservation of the constitution [and] the nation."

Key events began with one of Lincoln's earliest proclamations, which granted authority to his commanding general in Maryland, Winfield Scott, to do whatever necessary to counteract the open resistance that Union troops encountered in that area. By this point, mobs had attacked the Sixth Massachusetts Infantry as it traveled through Baltimore while heading south to Washington, DC. Meanwhile, the governor of Maryland had deployed the state militia and purportedly approved of the Baltimore mayor's orders that several key bridges be destroyed to thwart Union troop movements through the state. One of those believed to play a role in destroying several bridges was a Maryland farmer by the name of John Merryman, who was also an officer of the secessionist group the Baltimore County Horse Guards.

Pursuant to Scott's suspension, Union troops arrested Merryman, labeled him a traitor, and detained him at Fort McHenry. It does not appear that the government ever drew up a warrant for Merryman's arrest, likely because General George Cadwalader, the Union military commander in Maryland, did not believe that he needed one in light of the suspension.

But the government's position came to be tested. On the day of Merryman's arrest, one of his relatives drafted a habeas petition and arranged for its presentation in Washington to Chief Justice Taney. Within a couple of days, Taney traveled to Baltimore to hold a preliminary hearing on the matter, during which he held General Cadwalader in contempt for failing to appear. (Cadwalader had instead sent a deputy to explain the general's position that he had acted properly under the suspension and to assert that any judicial inquiry into the matter was improper.)

The next day, Tuesday, May 28, 1861, Chief Justice Taney made quick work of Cadwalader's argument, announcing his decision before a packed Baltimore courtroom. Taney rejected the position that the president could suspend habeas on his own and the idea that a civilian could otherwise be detained by military authorities. A few days later, Taney followed up with a lengthy written opinion in which he all but ridiculed the president's position, observing that "if the president of the United States may suspend the writ, then the constitution of the United States has conferred upon him more regal and absolute power over the liberty of the citizen, than the people of England have thought it safe to entrust to the crown." Taney relied heavily on English habeas tradition, detailing the events that led to the adoption of the English Habeas Corpus Act of 1679, including the arrest of John Selden, whose detention without criminal charges in the Tower of London had both laid the groundwork and highlighted the need for habeas legislation in the seventeenth century. "It is worthy of remark," Taney wrote, "that the offences…relied on as a justification for [Merryman's] arrest and imprisonment, in their nature and character, and in the loose and vague manner in which they are stated, bear a striking resemblance to those assigned in the warrant for the arrest of Mr. Selden."

But, Taney emphasized, the Habeas Corpus Act had addressed such failings: "The great and inestimable value of the habeas corpus act of the 31 Car. II. is, that it contains provisions which compel courts and judges, and all parties concerned, to perform their duties promptly, in the manner specified in the statute." That "manner" or tradition, Taney explained, formed the basis of American habeas law and established two important benchmarks of constitutional law. First, only the legislative body possesses the power to suspend habeas. Second, in the absence of a valid suspension, the government must charge someone like Merryman with a crime and try him in due course. If it fails to do so, a court is duty bound to order the prisoner's discharge. Thus, Taney held, because the government had failed to charge Merryman with a crime, his detention violated the Constitution. The chief justice concluded his opinion by noting that he had arranged for it to be delivered to President Lincoln personally.

Eventually, the Lincoln administration responded by indicting Merryman on criminal charges, including treason, though for various reasons, the government never proceeded with the prosecution. Notwithstanding this development, the president openly rejected Taney's *Merryman* opinion as wrong and proclaimed numerous additional suspensions over the course of the next two years. Lincoln also generally defended the president's unilateral power to suspend, asserting that "it was not believed that any law was violated." For good measure, Lincoln's attorney general, Edward Bates, also defended Lincoln's actions before Congress. Meanwhile, popular interest in the matter was extensive, and *Merryman* spearheaded the publication of a host of pamphlets taking sides on the question whether suspension is an executive or legislative power.

In the end, *Merryman* stands as a rare judicial rebuke of a president in wartime, albeit one written by a Supreme Court justice who is not especially well regarded in the annals of American history. (Chief Justice Taney drafted the slavery-supporting *Dred Scott* decision, one of the worst judicial decisions in American history.) In defense of Taney's position, one could cite English legal history in this context, which chronicles how suspension was by its origins a legislative power, the profound influence that history wielded over American habeas jurisprudence and the Suspension Clause, and the placement of the Suspension Clause in the legislative article of the US Constitution. One could also note the American founding generation's deep suspicion of executive power. But one must here confront Lincoln's defense of his actions as necessary to save the Union. As he wrote of his actions, "Often a limb must be amputated to save a life; but a life is never wisely given to save a limb. I felt that measures, otherwise unconstitutional, might become lawful, by becoming indispensable to the preservation of the constitution, through the preservation of the nation." Of course, the entire debate could have been avoided had Congress not waited two years in the face of a civil war tearing apart the Union before it finally passed suspension legislation.

Notably, President Lincoln appreciated other lessons derived from Anglo-American tradition. Specifically, he recognized that suspension was a necessary predicate for legalizing arrests that otherwise would be unconstitutional in the ordinary course. In a widely published letter, Lincoln wrote that the purpose of suspension was so that "men may be held in custody whom the courts acting on ordinary rules, would discharge." Lincoln further explained, "Habeas Corpus, does not discharge men who are proved to be guilty of defined crime; and its suspension is allowed by the constitution on purpose that, men may be arrested and held, who can not be proved to be guilty of defined crime, 'when in cases of Rebellion or Invasion the public Safety may require it.'" In these dire circumstances, Lincoln posited, "arrests are made, not so much for what has been done, as for what probably would be done." Ultimately, Lincoln suggested that "the time [is] not unlikely to come when I shall be blamed for having made too few arrests rather than too many."

In 1863, Congress finally enacted suspension legislation. Part of what spurred Congress to act was a push from the executive branch to do so, driven by concerns over a large number of lawsuits that had been brought against federal officials for false imprisonment during the ongoing war. Congress's response provided that "during the present rebellion, the President of the United States, whenever, in his judgment, the public safety may require it, is authorized to suspend the privilege of the writ of habeas corpus in any case throughout the United States, or any part thereof." By using the phrase "is authorized" rather than "is hereby authorized," Congress purposely declined to take a position on whether the president's actions to date had been legal, thereby side-stepping one of the major constitutional debates of the time and offering some legal cover to the government officer-defendants in the pending false imprisonment suits. But even as Congress authorized suspension in broad terms, it qualified its delegation. In its second section, the 1863 act required that lists of prisoners in custody be provided to the relevant local federal courts where they were open and operating. The section further provided that any prisoners in such areas should be discharged if the next sitting grand jury failed to indict them on formal criminal charges.

President Lincoln responded to the 1863 act by declaring a nationwide suspension applicable to all those held in military custody "either as prisoners of war, spies, or aiders or abettors of the enemy." It is notable that in so doing, Lincoln cited the 1863 act as the basis of his authority, possibly conceding that he had acted improperly before Congress vested him with the power to suspend. In all events, Lincoln's reference to "prisoners of war" likely encompassed Confederate soldiers already in custody or who would be taken into custody. After all, as English legal history had instructed, there was no need for a suspension to reach true prisoners of war, who were enemies in the service of a foreign sovereign. But to treat domestic prisoners "like other prisoners of war," as Lord North had declared in introducing the Revolutionary War suspension, did require a suspension. Because Lincoln believed that all persons supporting and fighting for the Confederacy still owed allegiance to the Union, this meant that the Union needed a suspension to hold them in a preventive posture. (Congress's legislation also spoke of this category of prisoners and exempted them from the requirements set forth in the second section of the act.)

Over the course of the war, the government detained thousands of Confederate soldiers as well as civilians in military custody. With a suspension in place, there was no legal obligation to try anyone as a basis for their continuing detention, except as the second section of the 1863 act required. The government only ever tried a portion of those held during the war for criminal conduct and, in a great number of cases, those trials occurred before military tribunals—a practice that implicates a host of additional constitutional issues. Meanwhile, it appears that the government failed to comply with the requirements of the second section of the act with very few, if any, exceptions. Ultimately, Lincoln's suspension remained operative in some states as late as a full year after Confederate General Robert E. Lee surrendered to Union General Ulysses S. Grant at Appomattox Court House. It was not until

6. A Union soldier guards Confederate prisoners at a prisoner of war camp.

1866 that Lincoln's successor, President Andrew Johnson, finally lifted the last of the Civil War suspension's applications.

The year 1866 also witnessed the Supreme Court decide the case of Ex parte *Milligan*, holding by a slim majority of 5–4 that the laws of war could not be applied to "citizens in states which have upheld the authority of the government, and where the courts are open and their process unobstructed." In such areas, the court held, civilians must be tried by regular courts and afforded the full panoply of constitutional rights relating to criminal procedure, including a jury trial. The court rejected the government's argument that military tribunals were lawful because the Bill of Rights were "peace provisions" that "like all other conventional and legislative laws and enactments, are silent amidst arms, and when the safety of the people becomes the supreme law." In an oft-quoted passage, the majority responded: "The Constitution of the United States is a law for rulers and people, equally in war and in peace, and covers with the shield of its protection all classes of men, at all times, and under all circumstances." (Four members of the *Milligan* court declined to sign on to such sweeping statements, concluding instead that Congress had the power to authorize military trials of civilians. Congress wasted little time in responding by authorizing military tribunals to do just that. With the war winding down, however, the Supreme Court never had occasion to confront the question whether congressional authorization of military trials in this context changed the constitutional calculus.)

In determining that Milligan's trial before a military commission was unconstitutional, the court also rejected the argument that the existence of a nationwide suspension had somehow rendered the trial legal. Suspension, the court held, only legalizes detention. It has no bearing on the propriety of military versus civilian courts, nor does it legitimate the denial of standard constitutional protections in the criminal process.

The *Milligan* decision has been chipped away in Supreme Court decisions rendered during World War II and more recently. There are also aspects of *Milligan* that are difficult to reconcile with the divided Supreme Court's decision early in the Civil War in the so-called *Prize Cases*. There, the court upheld Lincoln's invocation of various powers under the law of war to combat the secession of Southern states at the outset of the Civil War. The court's reasoning in the Prize Cases was based in part on the assumption that those who had sided with the South had "cast off their allegiance" to the Union, giving the war an international character. Thus, it is fair to say that Lincoln and the Supreme Court were not entirely consistent in their treatment of the concept of allegiance and the application of the law of war during the Civil War.

Regardless, President Lincoln established a sweeping historical precedent supporting the proposition that the executive could wield the dramatic suspension power unilaterally. A contemporaneous counterexample may be found in the experience of the short-lived Confederacy. For his part, Confederate President Jefferson Davis never acted ahead of his congress in declaring a suspension. Instead, he waited for the approval of the Confederate Congress before proclaiming three suspensions that governed in the Confederacy during periods of the war. The Confederate Congress also openly declared that suspension is exclusively a legislative power. The Reconstruction suspension that followed a few years later also witnessed Congress reclaim the power of suspension and a president who waited to exercise extraordinary detention authority until given a green light to do so by Congress. But in time, Lincoln's precedent of acting ahead of and apart from Congress would bear considerable fruit, most notably during World War II when President Franklin Delano Roosevelt came to invoke similar powers unilaterally, albeit without even bothering to proclaim a suspension.

Chapter 7
Reconstruction and expansion of the writ

In the wake of the Civil War, there was much work to be done to rebuild the Union. During this critical period in the United States, known as Reconstruction, the Constitution had to be reconceived to expand its protections to the newly freed slaves and address not just the threat posed by the federal government to individual liberties, which had been the focus of those who met in Philadelphia, but now also the threat posed by the states and individuals to those very same liberties. To that end, the Constitution added the Thirteenth, Fourteenth, and Fifteenth Amendments, ratified in 1865, 1868, and 1870, respectively. The Thirteenth Amendment prohibits "slavery" and "involuntary servitude." The Fourteenth Amendment promises citizenship to "all persons born or naturalized in the United States" and commands that "no State...shall abridge the privileges or immunities of citizens...; nor...deprive any person of life, liberty, or property, without due process of law; nor deny to any person within its jurisdiction the equal protection of the laws." And the Fifteenth Amendment guarantees that the "right of the citizens...to vote shall not be denied or abridged by the United States or by any State on account of race, color, or previous condition of servitude." In all three cases, the amendments bestow upon the US Congress the power to enforce their mandates. It is in this new chapter of American history that habeas corpus came—both through its expansion and, counterintuitively, through its suspension—to take on an outsized role in the promotion of civil rights.

As things unfolded, the profound alterations to the original compact known as the Reconstruction Amendments met dramatic resistance in many of the states that had once comprised the Confederacy. In many parts of the South, the Ku Klux Klan had become a domestic terrorist organization of tremendous consequence. The Klan brutally attacked African Americans and any who opposed the organization, while rendering some Southern states "unable to provide even the semblance of criminal law enforcement." This led former general and now president Ulysses S. Grant in March of 1871 "urgently" to recommend legislation to address the problem, conveying that it was "not clear" whether "the power of the Executive of the United States, acting within the limits of existing laws, is sufficient for present emergencies." The US Congress responded with the Ku Klux Klan Act of 1871. The act accomplished many things. First, it created a civil cause of action for "any person" deprived by a state actor of "any rights, privileges, or immunities secured by the Constitution." (This provision lives on in the early twenty-first century as 42 U.S.C. § 1983, an enormously important civil cause of action for enforcing civil rights.) Second, the 1871 act criminalized a range of conduct threatening civil rights. Finally, the act empowered the executive to employ the militia to suppress "insurrection[s], domestic violence, or combinations" and to "suspend the privileges of the writ of habeas corpus" to put down any "rebellion" orchestrated by "unlawful combinations" and designed to "overthrow or set at defiance the constituted authorities."

The act contained similar reporting requirements to those found in the second section of Congress's 1863 Civil War suspension. But unlike its predecessor, the 1871 act contained a sunset provision to ensure that its grant of dramatic powers to the executive would not extend beyond the period of critical need. This was necessary because, as Grant himself put it, the act conferred upon him "extraordinary powers." The president pledged that he would invoke those powers only "reluctant[ly]" and "in cases of imperative necessity…for the purpose of securing to all citizens…enjoyment of the rights guaranteed to them by the Constitution and laws."

Grant wasted little time in wielding his new authority. Knowing that he did not have sufficient military forces to blanket the South, Grant concentrated efforts on South Carolina and a key Klan stronghold in its upcountry. Grant first ordered Klan members in the area to disperse and turn over all weapons to federal authorities. When, unsurprisingly, his orders went unheeded, Grant proclaimed a suspension of "the privileges of the writ of *habeas corpus*" in nine upcountry counties. The suspension encompassed "all persons" arrested by federal officers in the area who were charged with violating the criminal provisions of the 1871 act. Mass arrests of presumed members of the Klan followed, along with military detention of the same. In the short term, the government's military commander in the area reported that the arrests had helped restore order. But when Congress permitted the suspension to lapse, the Klan quickly returned to its old ways. This is because only a handful of the many arrested and detained by the government were ever tried for criminal conduct, and by 1873, in keeping with a new policy of appeasement, Grant had offered all those swept up in the arrests either clemency or pardons.

Although of limited effect, the Reconstruction suspension is significant for several reasons. To begin, it marked the first time that a government had wielded suspension as a tool for promoting and protecting civil rights. President Grant invoked his extraordinary powers for the express purpose of trying to make real the constitutional rights that the Reconstruction Amendments had granted African Americans. Heretofore, suspension had always been viewed as at odds with the preservation of individual liberty. (To be sure, here, those members of the Klan who were arrested and detained under Grant's proclamation saw their rights implicated.) In addition, as had been the case during earlier periods, everyone appears to have understood during this period that once the suspension lapsed, those in custody could no longer be detained outside the criminal process. Accordingly, when the Reconstruction suspension expired, many of those in custody were referred for prosecution, while the government released all others.

The Reconstruction suspension, like the 1863 Civil War suspension, also witnessed Congress delegate the ultimate decision whether to suspend to the president. These examples contrast with the suspension proposed to address the Burr conspiracy, which suspended the privilege outright, as well as the final suspension enacted by the Confederate Congress during the Civil War, which by its terms suspended the privilege throughout the Confederacy after declaring that "the power of suspending the privilege . . . is vested solely in the Congress, which is the exclusive judge of the necessity of such suspension." There are good arguments both for and against the practice of a legislative delegation of the ultimate decision whether and where to suspend and for how long. Delegation could, for example, result in a narrowly targeted suspension, as happened during Reconstruction. But it bears noting that the practice was not known to Anglo-American tradition prior to the Civil War.

In all events, when the dust had settled and it came time to evaluate the Reconstruction suspension after it had lapsed, Congress studied its work. In so doing, that body concluded "that where the membership, mysteries, and power of the organization have been kept concealed [suspension] is the most and perhaps only effective remedy for its suppression." The Reconstruction example therefore also stands as one in which suspension served as a potent tool for infiltrating a highly secretive organization to uncover its structure and membership, although with the benefit of historical hindsight, one may question whether the government went far enough.

Meanwhile, the Reconstruction period witnessed the Supreme Court reaffirm the importance of the English Habeas Corpus Act as the foundation of the US Constitution's suspension clause. In an important habeas case decided during this period, Ex parte *Yerger*, the Supreme Court lauded the Habeas Corpus Act for "firmly guarantee[ing]" the "Great Writ." Continuing, the court observed that the act "was brought to America by the colonists, and claimed as among the immemorial rights descended to them from their ancestors," who in turn gave it "prominent sanction in the Constitution." But as will be seen, as the United States entered a new century, this long-recognized connection between the English act and the Suspension Clause came to be forgotten.

The Reconstruction period also witnessed another new chapter in the story of the writ. In keeping with the profound shift in the Constitution's focus during this period on the states, the US Congress dramatically expanded the office of habeas corpus in American law. In 1867, Congress enacted legislation vesting broad jurisdiction in the federal courts to review habeas petitions of those held in state custody. The context in which Congress took up the law, as well as its legislative history, reveals that Congress intended the new legislation to benefit the newly freed slaves by empowering them to challenge various state abuses directed at undermining their path to freedom. As one House resolution leading up to the 1867 act proclaimed, such legislation was needed "to enforce the liberty of all persons under the operation of the constitutional amendment abolishing slavery." Another immediate concern was the protection of federal officials from recalcitrant state governments.

Whether the 1867 Congress intended the law to sweep more broadly remains the subject of debate to this day. Either way, as enacted, the 1867 legislation made habeas corpus generally available to any person "restrained of his or her liberty in violation of the constitution, or of any treaty or law of the United States." With this legislation, Congress harnessed the habeas writ that abolitionist states had once wielded to protect fugitive slaves from federal authority, empowering the federal courts (once the enemy of freedom in this context) to employ the writ to protect the former slave's newfound freedom and rights.

Over time, the 1867 legislation proved the basis for another dramatic expansion of the concept of habeas corpus. Relying on the act's expansive language, federal courts began to exercise jurisdiction to review the petitions of those imprisoned following criminal conviction in state court. Until Reconstruction, those prosecuted in state criminal proceedings could only obtain federal court review of their convictions through direct appeal to the Supreme Court of the United States. But under an expanded conception of habeas corpus, state prisoners came to challenge their convictions and imprisonment as violating federal law both on direct appeal to the Supreme Court and subsequently in federal court through one or two avenues of habeas proceedings. First, a state prisoner could appeal to the Supreme Court from a secondary round of litigation in state courts challenging a conviction (or what are commonly referred to as state collateral or state habeas proceedings). Second, a state prisoner could separately or subsequently pursue habeas relief in the lower federal courts (in what is known as collateral federal court habeas proceedings), with the ability to appeal any decision to the Supreme Court.

This expansion did not happen overnight. An early example of the resistance met by attempts to expand federal habeas may be found in the 1915 case of *Frank v. Magnum*. The petition in the case had been filed in federal district court and then appealed to the Supreme Court. The high court denied relief to the petitioner who claimed, with considerable evidence, that his trial had been dominated by a mob and he therefore had been denied due process of law. In dissent, Justice Oliver Wendell Holmes, Jr., argued that "mob law does not become due process of law by securing the assent of a terrorized jury." Nor, he contended, should federal courts treat the state court's resolution of the matter as unreviewable. "Where the processes of justice are actually subverted," he wrote, "the federal court has jurisdiction to issue the writ."

Although on the losing end in *Frank v. Magnum*, Justice Holmes took the reins eight years later when the court decided *Moore v. Dempsey*, another case involving mob domination of state criminal proceedings. The case involved the prosecution of several African American men for the alleged murder of a white man in Arkansas. Echoing his dissent in *Frank*, Holmes reasoned that if "the whole proceeding is a mask [and] counsel, jury and judge were swept to the fatal end by an irresistible wave of public passion, and . . . the State Courts failed to correct the wrong," the state had denied the petitioners due process of law. In Holmes's view, moreover, it was for federal habeas courts to enforce such rights against the state.

Over time, the federal courts built on Holmes's vision and expanded collateral habeas review to encompass not only claims attacking the jurisdiction of a convicting court and the provision of basic due process, but also constitutional claims more generally. This shift coincided with a decline in direct Supreme Court review on appeal of state criminal convictions, and there is evidence to suggest that it was part of a conscious decision by the high court to shift federal court review of state criminal convictions from its docket to the lower federal courts. The high-water mark of this new vision for habeas came in 1953, when the Supreme Court decided *Brown v. Allen* and held that state prisoners may obtain a full airing of constitutional claims challenging state criminal convictions in collateral federal habeas corpus proceedings. As Justice Felix Frankfurter explained in his concurring opinion in the case (an opinion that in time came to be regarded as the primary opinion for the court), "by giving the federal courts [this] jurisdiction [in 1867], Congress has imbedded into federal legislation the historic function of habeas corpus adapted to reaching an enlarged area of claims." Any such review, moreover, was to be undertaken on a de novo basis—that is, on a blank slate—because, as Frankfurter put it, "the prior State determination of a claim under the United States Constitution cannot foreclose consideration of such a claim, else the State court would have the final say which the Congress, by the Act of 1867, provided it should not have."

The result of this expansion has been dramatic. Through habeas cases appealed from state collateral proceedings and others originating in the lower federal courts, the Supreme Court of the United States has handed down some of its most important constitutional law decisions in the criminal law context. These include, to name but a few, *Gideon v. Wainwright* (1963), holding that the Sixth Amendment requires state courts to appoint attorneys for criminal defendants who cannot afford to retain counsel on their own; *Brady v. Maryland* (1963), holding that prosecutors must turn over evidence favorable to a criminal defendant that is material to guilt or punishment; *Ford v. Wainwright* (1986), holding that the Eighth Amendment and due process prohibit the imposition of the death penalty upon the insane; and *Roper v. Simmons* (2005), holding that the Eighth Amendment prohibits the execution of minors.

Meanwhile, history has also witnessed the limitation of habeas as a means of securing a more just criminal system. Examples on this score, to name but a few, include *Frank v. Magnum*; *Stone v. Powell* (1976), holding that Fourth Amendment challenges to the acquisition of evidence for a state criminal prosecution are generally unreviewable in federal habeas proceedings; and *McCleskey v. Kemp* (1987), which declined to rule the death penalty unconstitutional in the face of statistics showing racial disparities in the awarding of the sentence.

Habeas has also fallen short as a means of challenging ongoing criminal prosecutions, even when supported by strong arguments that a prosecution is unjust. This is a lesson that suffragist Susan B. Anthony learned the hard way in 1873 when she sought a writ of habeas corpus in federal district court, seeking to prevent her prosecution for violating federal voting laws. The court to which she petitioned declined to intervene and the government soon thereafter convicted Anthony for voting illegally, after which she was fined one hundred dollars. (She never paid the fine, and the government did not pursue the matter.)

In more recent decades, the scope of collateral habeas relief has contracted considerably. This trend began with a number of judicial decisions that walked back *Brown v. Allen*'s broad vision for collateral habeas, including *Stone v. Powell* and *Teague v. Lane* (1989), which precluded habeas petitioners from benefiting from any new court decisions rendered after a criminal defendant has exhausted all direct appeals. Congress also took up new legislation in 1996, enacting the Antiterrorism and Effective Death Penalty Act, or AEDPA, as it is commonly known. Codifying many of the intervening judicial decisions, AEDPA also went further to scale back the availability of collateral federal court habeas review of state court convictions. Thus, AEDPA introduced for the first time a statute of limitations that governs collateral petitions brought in federal court (a period of one year, running from the date of finality of a defendant's appeals), limits the ability to file second or successive collateral habeas petitions, curtails the opportunity to obtain hearings to introduce new evidence in habeas proceedings, and requires federal courts to defer to "reasonable" holdings rendered by state courts with respect to federal constitutional claims. As the Supreme Court explained in the 2011 case of *Harrington v. Richter*, AEDPA's deferential standard requires a prisoner to show that a state court's ruling on his or her claims "was so lacking in justification that there was any error well understood and comprehended in existing law beyond any possibility for fairminded disagreement."

Under this standard, in the early twenty-first century it is a rare occasion when a state prisoner satisfies AEDPA and secures relief from a federal habeas court. For this reason, some have argued that many aspects of AEDPA transgress constitutional boundaries. In one early case interpreting the statute, *Williams v. Taylor* (2000), Supreme Court Justice John Paul Stevens argued that AEDPA's provision requiring deference to state court decisions on constitutional claims that are "reasonable," yet contrary to the conclusion a federal court would reach in its own independent judgment, violates the separation of powers and judicial independence. But Justice Stevens was on the losing end of the argument; in *Williams*, a court majority upheld AEDPA's standard of deference. To date, the Supreme Court has broadly interpreted and routinely upheld many of AEDPA's provisions, resulting in a dramatic drop in the number of habeas cases winning relief under this framework. (Notably, AEDPA does not apply and therefore does not require the Supreme Court to defer in any fashion to state courts when it rules on issues arising in cases coming to it on appeal from state habeas courts.) Many scholars and judges have argued that AEDPA undermines the role of habeas corpus in securing a fair and impartial criminal justice system. More generally, some have questioned, in light of AEDPA's deference requirements, whether the vision at the heart of the writ of habeas corpus—namely, that the "judge judges"—can be reconciled with this model of habeas.

Chapter 8
World War II and the demise of the Great Writ

The bombing of Pearl Harbor on December 7, 1941, finally ushered the United States into World War II. The US Congress declared war on Japan the next day. It then declared war on Germany three days later. The attack on Pearl Harbor set off a dramatic chain of events both in the Hawaiian Territory and on the mainland of the United States. Suspension and martial law came to rule in Hawaii, while in the Western mainland United States a series of military orders ultimately sought to control the movements of, and in time detain, approximately 120,000 Japanese Americans. Those incarcerated under military orders during this period included more than 70,000 US citizens.

The United States was not alone in targeting its own citizens for detention. Across the Atlantic, Great Britain declared war on Germany in September 1939 after Germany's invasion of Poland. After Germany invaded France the following year, the British government adopted Regulation 18B of the wartime Defence (General) Regulations to empower the executive to detain British citizens believed to pose a danger to national security. In contrast to the staggering numbers of Japanese Americans detained during the war in the United States, the Home Office interned just shy of two thousand British citizens under Regulation 18B during the same period. When the program commenced, Prime Minister Winston Churchill had been an enthusiastic supporter. (Speaking at the start of the war of enemies discovered within Great Britain, for example, Churchill had proclaimed, "Collar the lot!") In time, however, his opposition to the program would play an important role in its termination.

As these events unfolded on both sides of the Atlantic, the principles of the English Habeas Corpus Act of 1679—so long the foundation of habeas jurisprudence and a constraint on executive detention in both countries—came to be severely tested.

The American experience during the war

In the immediate wake of the attack on Pearl Harbor, Hawaiian territorial governor Joseph Poindexter declared a suspension of habeas corpus and proclaimed martial law on the islands. To do so, he invoked the Hawaiian Organic Act of 1900, which delegated to the governor standing authority to suspend the privilege "in case of rebellion or invasion, or imminent danger thereof, when the public safety requires it," along with the power to "place the Territory, or any part thereof, under martial law." Under the act, any suspension or declaration of martial law would remain in effect "until communication [could] be had with the President and his decision thereon made known." President Roosevelt quickly approved the governor's actions, and this state of affairs on the islands governed through much of the war.

Following the governor's proclamation, the military took over all governmental affairs in Hawaii, including the courts, and eliminated trial by jury while declaring that all criminal trials be conducted by military tribunals. The latter practice continued even after civilian courts reopened later in the war to hear noncriminal matters. Under the auspices of the suspension, the military arrested citizens suspected of disloyalty and detained them without formal hearings and without criminal charges. The military also issued orders prohibiting the filing or even acceptance by a judge of a petition for a writ of habeas corpus.

Nonetheless, the US District Court for the territory of Hawaii decided several notable habeas cases during the war. It did so in two contexts: first, challenges to arrests and detentions for so-called subversive activities; and second, challenges to military criminal trials. In both contexts, habeas petitioners argued that the military's exercise of emergency powers transgressed the Constitution, the Hawaiian Organic Act, or both. After the war, the Supreme Court reviewed many of these actions in *Duncan v. Kahanamoku* (1946) and held unlawful the government's declaration of martial law in the Hawaiian Islands, ultimately vacating the convictions of two civilians who had been tried by a military commission for embezzlement and assault. (Notably, the decision was grounded in an interpretation of the Hawaiian Organic Act, although the Constitution loomed large over the majority opinion written by Justice Hugo Black.)

The story on the mainland in the United States was very different, though it led to similar results. There, Congress never debated, much less passed, any suspension legislation. Instead, military orders carrying out President Franklin Delano Roosevelt's infamous Executive Order 9066 governed the treatment of those suspected of potential disloyalty. Executive Order 9066, which President Roosevelt issued on February 19, 1942—ten weeks after the Japanese attack on Pearl Harbor—authorized the secretary of war to designate military zones "from which any or all persons may be excluded" and regulate the terms by which persons could enter, remain in, or be forced to leave such areas. By its own terms, 9066 included no language specifically targeting a particular group. Nor did the order expressly mention detention, but it did authorize the secretary of war "to provide for residents of any such area who are excluded therefrom, such transportation, food, shelter, and other accommodations as may be necessary."

In the months following issuance of 9066, the military imposed curfews, designated large swaths of the Western United States as military areas of exclusion, and ultimately built detention camps across the West in which it detained thousands of Japanese Americans for an average stay of three years. By their terms, the regulations, issued under the pen of the commanding general of the Western Defense Command, John L. DeWitt, targeted alien enemies and "all persons of Japanese ancestry," whether citizens or not.

In the lead-up to 9066, key government officials knew or, in the case of President Roosevelt, had been counseled that any detention of Japanese American citizens would violate the Suspension Clause of the US Constitution. Roosevelt's attorney general, Francis Biddle, repeatedly took this position with the president and members of Congress, saying at one point, "Unless the Writ of Habeas Corpus is suspended, I do not know of any way in which Japanese born in this country and therefore American citizens could be interned." Secretary of War Henry L. Stimson wrote in his diary during this period that "we cannot discriminate among our citizens on the ground of racial origin." One of the lawyers privately counseling President Roosevelt during this time, moreover, conveyed to him that implementing the proposed removal and detention of Japanese Americans "would probably require suspension of the writ of habeas corpus."

Further, in the weeks before the president issued 9066, military reports concluded, and high-ranking War and Justice Department officials recognized, that there existed no evidence of widespread disloyalty justifying any plan to disturb Japanese American citizens. Just days before the issuance of 9066, Attorney General Biddle informed Roosevelt that the Justice Department "believed mass evacuation at this time inadvisable [because] there were no reasons for mass evacuation." Referring to newspaper columnists who were aggressively advocating for the internment of Japanese Americans, Biddle told the president that either they "ha[ve] information which the War Department and the F.B.I. apparently do not have, or [they are] acting with dangerous irresponsibility."

Consistent with these conclusions was a report prepared for the chief of naval operations by Lieutenant Commander Kenneth D. Ringle in January 1942 that argued that the so-called "'Japanese Problem' [had] been magnified out of its true proportion" and reported that "the most dangerous" were already in custody or "known" to Naval Intelligence and/or the FBI. Even FBI director J. Edgar Hoover—himself no stranger to robust surveillance—believed that the push for internment was "based primarily upon public and political pressure rather than on factual data." (In 1983, a congressional commission charged with studying the episode likewise concluded that "no documented acts of espionage, sabotage or fifth column activity were shown to have been committed by any identifiable American citizen of Japanese ancestry or resident Japanese alien on the West Coast" in the period leading up to the military orders.)

But with 9066, Roosevelt gave the military, in the words of Assistant Secretary of War John J. McCloy, "carte blanche" to proceed as it saw fit. McCloy's comments on another occasion epitomized the War Department's approach to the entire matter. As he viewed things, "If it is a question of safety of the country, the Constitution of the United States, why the Constitution is just a scrap of paper to me."

And so it followed that General DeWitt issued a flurry of orders and the government quickly constructed "relocation centers" in barren and desolate areas primarily in the Western states, surrounding them with barbed wire fences and armed guards at all times. This historical episode has long been referred to as "the Japanese American internment." In the early twenty-first century, however, Japanese Americans promote the use of the terms incarceration and detention, rather than internment, in referring to the camps.

Those forced to live in the camps faced extreme conditions, little in the way of privacy, and substandard food and medical care. It

7. A Japanese American grandfather and his grandchildren wait for an evacuation bus in Hayward, California, on May 8, 1942. The bus will take them to the Tanforan Assembly Center, from which they will be sent to a "relocation center," or incarceration camp.

was not uncommon for the military to split families apart and send family members to different camps. Those subject to detention were permitted to take only what they could carry. As a result, Japanese Americans were forced to abandon their homes, stores, farms, and all belongings, or to sell them off quickly at a fraction of their worth. In short, most Japanese Americans on the West Coast lost everything, including years of their lives.

8. **Military police watch over the Santa Anita Assembly Center in Arcadia, California. Japanese Americans incarcerated during World War II by the US government spent an average of three years in various detention camps.**

To bolster 9066 and the War Department's regulations, the US Congress enacted legislation criminalizing violations of the military orders, rendering defiance something few people would risk. But some did nonetheless. A handful of Japanese American citizens violated the military orders and then challenged the entire 9066 infrastructure in their subsequent prosecutions. Three such cases eventually made their way to the Supreme Court of the United States, along with a separate habeas case that challenged outright the mass incarceration. In all four cases, the Supreme Court was at best unwilling to engage with the Constitution in evaluating the government's actions and at worst complicit in the gross constitutional violations that followed under 9066.

Gordon Hirabayashi's case, *Hirabayashi v. United States*, was the first to reach the court, in 1943. Hirabayashi, a senior at the

University of Washington and natural-born citizen whose parents had immigrated from Japan, had been prosecuted for violating local curfew orders and an order requiring that he register with military authorities, something that would surely have led to his detention in a camp. Hirabayashi argued that Congress had delegated excessive authority to General DeWitt and that DeWitt's orders unconstitutionally discriminated on the basis of race and ethnicity in violation of the Fifth Amendment of the US Constitution. It was to no avail. In upholding the orders, the Supreme Court observed, "The adoption by Government, in the crisis of war and of threatened invasion, of measures for the public safety, based upon the recognition of facts and circumstances which indicate that a group of one national extraction may menace that safety more than others, is not wholly beyond the limits of the Constitution and is not to be condemned merely because in other and in most circumstances racial distinctions are irrelevant." Meanwhile, the court also remanded a companion case, *Yasui v. United States*, to a lower federal court without questioning the authority of the military to issue curfew orders. Deference to the military ruled the day.

Next, in its 1944 decision in *Korematsu v. United States*, the Supreme Court upheld Fred Korematsu's conviction for violating an exclusion order by remaining in a designated military zone in Northern California. The court again declined to "reject as unfounded the judgment of the military authorities and of Congress that there were disloyal members of that population, whose number and strength could not be precisely and quickly ascertained." In *Korematsu*, however, the court was no longer unanimous in its deference to military authorities. One dissenter, Justice Owen Roberts, complained that the policies in question had resulted in Korematsu's "imprisonment in a concentration camp, based on his ancestry, and solely because of his ancestry, without evidence or inquiry concerning his loyalty and good disposition towards the United States." Another dissenter, Justice Robert Jackson, feared that the majority's opinion would lie "about like a loaded weapon ready for the hand of any authority that can bring forward a plausible claim of an urgent need." (To his point, *Korematsu* remained good law for decades until the Supreme Court overruled it in its 2018 *Trump v. Hawaii* decision, albeit in dictum—that is, in a part of the opinion that is not binding precedent for future cases because it was unnecessary to the underlying decision.)

In only one of these cases did the court side against the military during the war. That case, Ex parte *Endo*, proved an enormously important victory for Japanese Americans. *Endo* came down on December 18, 1944, the same day the court decided *Korematsu*. Mitsuye Endo was a US citizen who, following the attack on Pearl Harbor, had been fired by the state of California along with every other Japanese American employee. Next, she had been forced to evacuate the military area encompassing her hometown of Sacramento, California, ordered to report to an assembly center, and eventually detained in a camp with her family. Meanwhile, Endo's brother was serving in the US Army. In a petition for a writ of habeas corpus, Endo challenged her detention as unconstitutional. Endo relied on Ex parte *Milligan* and a host of additional historical precedents for the proposition that the government had no general authority to detain citizens without bringing criminal charges. Quoting extensively from *Milligan*, Endo's brief asked, "Since the military authorities have no jurisdiction by virtue of a Presidential proclamation to try a civilian for an alleged offense in a district where the civil Courts are open, how much less right have they to imprison a citizen without any trial at all, when he is neither charged with, nor suspected of, any crime, and when his loyalty (as in this case), is not called into question?"

Endo's case was the only direct challenge to the existence of the camps to reach the Supreme Court and is noteworthy for this fact alone. But there are additional aspects that highlight its extraordinary nature. To begin, the government attempted to moot her case as it made its way through the federal courts by offering Endo release on the condition that she relocate outside the evacuation areas. (Had she accepted, there would no longer have been a "body" in custody over which the habeas court could have exercised jurisdiction.) She refused.

When Endo's case finally made its way to the Supreme Court after a lengthy stay in the lower courts, she won, and that victory directly led to the closing of the camps. But she won only on very narrow grounds. Specifically, the court held that the military regulations required the release of concededly loyal citizens from relocation centers. (The government had long conceded Endo's loyalty as part of its efforts to convince her to accept release and moot her case.) By deciding the case on such limited grounds and granting Endo the relief she sought (release), the court avoided reaching any of the constitutional issues weighing in the balance.

Under the court's holding, the concept of loyalty loomed large. Nonetheless, the court failed to say anything about how loyalty should be determined. Nor had earlier cases ever defined the concept. This is because "loyalty" had never been relevant to habeas and Suspension Clause jurisprudence, the focus of which in this context had always asked whether the government offered a speedy trial on criminal charges in the absence of a suspension and nothing further.

Internal court documents suggest that Chief Justice Harlan Fiske Stone, knowing that the court would decide the case unanimously in Endo's favor, held up the decision to give President Roosevelt time to act ahead of the court and withdraw 9066. Roosevelt had also won reelection in the meantime, and historians have documented how he moderated his resistance to closing the camps only after the election. On December 17, 1944, Major General Henry C. Pratt issued Public Proclamation No. 21, which declared that as of January 2, 1945, all Japanese American evacuees were free to return to their homes on the West Coast.

The court handed down *Endo* the next day. In the weeks that followed, the government began the process of closing the camps. At the time—three years after the attacks on Pearl Harbor—the camps still detained eighty-five thousand Japanese Americans. Endo may not have established an important constitutional law precedent, but her habeas case closed the camps.

Assessment of these cases along with the treatment of Japanese Americans during World War II has focused predominantly on the discriminatory components of the government's actions. It is easy to understand why. There is a wealth of evidence documenting that discrimination played an enormous role in the adoption of the military policies targeting Japanese Americans. But in all of this, it is important to recognize that the incarceration of Japanese Americans also stands as a massive violation of the Suspension Clause.

The British experience during the war

In the wake of American independence, British habeas jurisprudence continued to embrace a suspension model grounded in the English Habeas Corpus Act. But just as in the United States, that model came under tremendous pressure in the twentieth century in Great Britain.

The evolution of British habeas jurisprudence is rooted in the fact that in Great Britain, there is no codified constitution. Instead, as the Supreme Court of the United Kingdom observed in 2017 in the first of two decisions respecting matters related to Britain's exit from the European Union, "Parliamentary sovereignty is a fundamental principle of the UK constitution." Thus, because the Habeas Corpus Act was a parliamentary creation, it was always the case that Parliament could suspend the act—as it did on many occasions—or modify or even repeal it through ordinary legislation. Until the twentieth century, when Parliament believed that the Habeas Corpus Act's protections would obstruct the needs of national security, it turned to suspension. This practice culminated in suspensions applicable to Ireland in 1866 and 1867. But during both world wars, Parliament charted a very different course. Instead of turning to suspension as a tool for expanding executive authority or tinkering with the Habeas Corpus Act itself, during both wars, Parliament authorized the executive in sweeping terms to detain suspected domestic enemies of the state in the absence of a suspension.

Parliament did so through general wartime legislation in which it granted a host of emergency powers to the executive. During World War I, executive detention authority followed under Regulation 14B, issued under the auspices of the Defence of the Realm Act, which granted the executive extensive authority to "issue regulations for securing the public safety and the defence of the realm." Promulgated in June 1915, Regulation 14B authorized the detention of British subjects of "hostile origin or associations." The government denied those swept up within 14B's framework the right to trial for the duration of their internment.

In the 1917 case of *R. v. Halliday*, a German-born naturalized British citizen argued in a habeas petition that his detention under Regulation 14B was unlawful. Rejecting his arguments, the Law Lords—the highest law court in Britain during this period—upheld the legality of the internment program by reading the governing legislation as granting the government broad powers, including the authority to do whatever was necessary to protect the home front. The concurring opinion of Lord John Atkinson summarizes the Lords' mentality in the case: "However precious the personal liberty of the subject may be, there is something for which it may well be, to some extent, sacrificed by legal enactment, namely, national success in the war, or escape from national plunder or enslavement."

A similar story unfolded during World War II. When Great Britain entered the war, just as in the United States, the government first targeted enemy aliens for detention. Soon, however, Prime Minister Winston Churchill expressed his enthusiasm for using any and all government powers to stamp out "Fifth Column" activities—that is, the actions of those at home who supported the enemy. This included exercising the power to detain suspected subversive citizens. Pursuant to Parliament's 1939 Emergency Powers (Defence) Act, the Privy Council built on the precedent of Regulation 14B and adopted Regulation 18B, authorizing the detention of British citizens suspected of being under foreign influence or otherwise involved in Fifth Column activities.

After Parliament rejected the initial version of Regulation 18B for granting the secretary of state unfettered discretion, an amended version of Regulation 18B provided that where the secretary believed it was "necessary to exercise control over [a person]," he could order an arrest based on "reasonable cause" to believe that a person was "of hostile origin or associations or [had] been recently concerned in acts prejudicial to the public safety or the defence of the realm or in the preparation or instigation of such acts." In May 1940, Regulation 18B was amended once again to expand its reach to persons who were or had been members or allies of various subversive organizations.

Over the course of its implementation, Regulation 18B led to the arrest and detention of almost two thousand British citizens, including a member of Parliament as well as two of Prime Minister Churchill's cousins by marriage. The second amended version of 18B prodded the Home Office to target members of the British Union of Fascists and other organizations, including the Irish Republican Army. Detentions reached their height in the summer of 1940 when, according to the home secretary, the government had increased the number of detainees by approximately thirteen hundred people. With each year of the war, however, the number of detainees dropped precipitously, falling to under one hundred by 1944. The day following VE Day,

May 8, 1945, an Order in Council permitted Regulation 18B to lapse.

As required by Regulation 18B, the Home Office appointed advisory panels for reviewing the basis of detention orders soon after Regulation 18B went into effect. Even though the Home Office established four panels to review cases, there were already major backlogs in 1940. Despite the delays, evidence suggests that at times the panels exercised their responsibility with some care. For example, there were four days of hearings held in the high-profile case of Sir Oswald Mosley, a former member of Parliament and the leader of the British Union of Fascists. Reports nonetheless suggest that in most cases, hearings were brief and mainly involved interrogations of those detained.

Over the course of 18B's existence, the advisory committee also recommended the release of a substantial number of detainees. But the home secretary retained the authority to disregard the recommendations of the advisory committee and he did so on several occasions, despite acknowledging in the summer of 1940 "the possibility that some mistakes may have been made" under the Regulation 18B scheme. This being said, in a deeply unpopular decision that triggered extensive public backlash, the home secretary authorized the release of Mosley. Defending his decision, the secretary observed, "When the tumult and the shouting have died down this decision to release a man detested by the entire British community, to release him…because it would be constitutionally wrong to detain him, may well teach critics in some other countries—critics who seem to stand in need of the lesson—the genuine meaning of democracy in a community mature enough to know its own spirit and its own mind."

In time, some of those held under Regulation 18B sought refuge in the British courts, meeting no more success than those who had done so during World War I. The leading case from this period is *Liversidge v. Anderson*, which reached the Law Lords in the fall of

Put Mosley back in Jail !

To the Prime Minister, 10 Downing Street, Whitehall, S.W.1.

WE, the undersigned, demand that Mosley be put back in jail immediately.

No pretexts or excuses can justify his release which we regard as an insult to the men and women in the fighting forces, their relatives and to all, who in any way are contributing to the defeat of Fascism.

9. British citizens posted many petitions supporting putting Sir Oswald Mosley back in jail in 1943 in response to his unpopular release from detention under the Regulation 18B regime in Great Britain during the war.

1941 and at a particularly low point in the war. Liversidge had sued the secretary for false imprisonment, arguing that the court should require the secretary to disclose the "particulars" of his "reasonable belief" that Liversidge qualified for detention under the terms of Regulation 18B. Four of the five Law Lords concluded that reviewing the secretary's actions required the courts to employ a subjective test, which led them to hold that the home secretary's belief that he had reasonable cause for suspecting Liversidge of hostile origins or association was sufficient to sustain the detention. In so doing, the majority declined to apply an objective test that may well have called into question the secretary's actions in some cases. In support of this approach, the majority observed that the Home Office likely made detention decisions based on confidential information. The result effectively left the executive with unchecked discretion to administer 18B.

In a dissenting opinion, Lord James Richard Atkin struck a very different chord, contending 18B's requirement of a "reasonable belief" on the part of the home secretary established an objective standard that courts could and should employ to review the secretary's asserted justifications in detentions cases. Atkin relied on the fact that the regulation had been amended to scale back the discretion it initially vested in the home secretary. Atkin continued by arguing more fundamentally that "the laws speak the same language in war as in peace." (Here, Atkin's words echoed those of the Supreme Court of the United States in Ex parte *Milligan* just after the Civil War.) Atkin further declared that "one of the principles of liberty for which . . . we are now fighting [is] that the judges . . . stand between the subject and any attempted encroachments on his liberty by the executive." Nodding to history, Atkin posited that "in this case I have listened to arguments which might have been addressed acceptably to the Court of King's Bench in the time of Charles I"—that is, before the reforms that included adoption of the English Habeas Corpus Act of 1679. But Atkin stood alone in dissent.

Thus, British courts effectively played no role in supervising or constraining the executive's detention powers under Regulation 18B. (Challenges to internment programs in Canada and Australia during the war met with similar judicial reluctance to intervene.) Instead, the pressure to wind down the 18B regime came from within the executive branch and from one person in particular— Winston Churchill. Over the course of the war, Churchill had become an increasingly staunch critic of Regulation 18B and its provision for the detention of citizens outside the criminal process. By the end of 1941, Churchill was already declaring that the powers vested in the executive by Regulation 18B should "be abandoned as soon as possible." And by the fall of 1943, Churchill had turned completely against 18B, admonishing that "the power of the Executive to cast a man into prison without formulating any charge known to the law, and particularly to deny him the judgement of his peers, is in the highest degree odious and is the foundation of all totalitarian government." Contemporaneously, Churchill also celebrated "the great principle of habeas corpus and trial by jury, which are the supreme protection invented by the British people for ordinary individuals against the State." This recognition of a robust habeas tradition ultimately led Churchill to urge the repeal of Regulation 18B, counseling that "such powers . . . are contrary to the whole spirit of British public life and British history." Putting these ideas together, Churchill advised his home secretary, "I am convinced 18.B should be completely abolished as the national emergency no longer justifies abrogation of individual rights of habeas corpus and trial by jury on definite charges."

Churchill did not care that his position went against the tide of popular and political support for the government's detention policies. Indeed, he urged the home secretary on all the same, advising him that "people who are not prepared to do unpopular things and to defy clamour are not fit to be Ministers in times of stress." Finally, in a passage that underscores Churchill's contemporary recognition of the historical precedent that his administration was establishing, he counseled the secretary that "any unpopularity you have incurred through correct and humane exercise of your functions will be repaid in a few months by public respect."

Lessons from the comparison

During the war, courts in both countries staked out roles that left them largely relegated to the sidelines. In the United States, this development proved a turning point in American constitutional habeas jurisprudence. The story is more complicated in the United Kingdom, where parliamentary supremacy was and remains the rule. Critics have nonetheless taken aim at the failure of British courts to review how the secretary exercised the authority under 18B. With the exception of Ex parte *Endo* in the United States, judicial deference in both countries left the executive essentially with unchecked discretion over individual liberty during the war.

Notably, however, as the war continued, the two chief executives struck markedly different positions on the wisdom and lawfulness of detention policies directed at citizens. In the United States, Roosevelt ignored the advice of many of his key advisers regarding the lack of need for and unconstitutionality of the detention of Japanese Americans. He also ignored his advisors in delaying the closing of the detention camps until after the 1944 election and learning of the government's loss in *Endo*. By contrast, Churchill led the charge to repeal Regulation 18B.

Other important differences existed between the British and American experiences during this period. To begin, Churchill operated within a constitutional tradition that often looked more to Parliament than the courts to protect individual liberty. Thus, it was not uncommon to see works on the British Constitution instruct, as Sir Ivor Jennings once wrote, that "the law is what Parliament provides, and it is in Parliament that the focus of our liberties must be found." In the United States, by contrast, the courts have always been thought to play an outsized role on this score. For example, at the founding, James Madison said that the courts "will consider themselves...the guardians of [constitutional] Rights" and "be an impenetrable bulwark against every assumption of power in the Legislature or Executive." And, a few decades later, Chief Justice John Marshall famously asserted in *Marbury v. Madison* that it is the role of the judiciary "to say what the law is."

Further, unlike Roosevelt, Churchill did not face a general election during the war, which insulated him considerably from popular pressures during this period. One is left to question whether Churchill would have yielded more to popular pressure regarding the 18B program had he been required to defend his position in an election.

Finally, those individuals swept up in detentions under Regulation 18B looked very different from those who were targeted by American policies. This point highlights that discrimination was at the heart of the detention policies that followed under 9066. It is well documented, moreover, that before, during, and even after the war, Japanese Americans experienced exclusion from full integration into American society and wielded little foothold in the political process. (Even the Supreme Court in *Hirabayashi* questioned the ability of Japanese Americans to assimilate into American society.) One is left to wonder whether the fact that Churchill had relatives swept up under 18B helped him better appreciate the dramatic impact on individual liberties that followed under the 18B regime.

Coming full circle, the British and American experiences reveal two important lessons. First, the detention policies that both countries adopted during the war underscore the waning influence of the English Habeas Corpus Act and the suspension framework that had long governed in Anglo-American habeas jurisprudence. The retreat in both countries from adherence to the constraints at the heart of the Habeas Corpus Act and, in the case of the United States, the Suspension Clause proved significant in the decades that followed in the face of a new threat to national security—terrorism.

Second, even taking into account distinctions between the two countries, Churchill's role in shutting down the 18B regime suggests that an executive can—even in times of war—take the lead in championing constitutional values. Roosevelt's actions, by contrast, stand as a cautionary tale on this score. Ultimately, an important lesson that emerges is one that US Supreme Court Justice Tom Clark recognized in writing about 9066 after the war. "Constitutions and laws are not sufficient of themselves," he wrote, but "must be given life through implementation and strict enforcement." Accordingly, it matters a great deal that government officials internalize constitutional principles, lest those principles and the document from which they derive be relegated to nothing more than "a scrap of paper."

Chapter 9
Habeas corpus today

In the early twenty-first century, the writ of habeas corpus plays several roles. In addition to serving as a vehicle for collateral review of criminal convictions, habeas also serves as the means by which courts evaluate a range of immigration matters as well as the legality of the detention of prisoners in modern armed conflicts, including most prominently the war on terrorism. (This list is by no means exclusive because habeas also plays many other roles, including evaluating extradition cases.) Studying how habeas functions in immigration and modern wartime detention cases reveals both the writ's potential and its limitations.

Immigration

The United States did not formally begin to restrict immigration to the country under federal law until 1875. Until then, the country maintained an "open door" policy to immigrants. Between 1875 and 1961, federal courts assumed jurisdiction to review immigration cases of those held in government custody under the 1867 Reconstruction-era habeas statute, which broadly provided for habeas review of those held in federal or state custody in violation of federal law. Through such review, courts inquired whether an individual was being detained in violation of the immigration laws.

One early habeas case in this context was *United States v. Jung Ah Lung*, decided by the Supreme Court in 1888. The petitioner, a Chinese immigrant laborer, had lived in the United States but left to visit China. When he returned to the United States without the papers he needed for re-entry, which he had lost, immigration authorities refused to admit him and detained him. Concluding he had a lawful right to enter the country, a district court ordered his release into the United States, a decision affirmed by the Supreme Court. Congress responded by passing new immigration legislation in 1891 that purported to restrict judicial review of immigration proceedings and render them "final." In the 1892 case of *Nishimura Ekiu v. United States*, the Supreme Court interpreted the new statute to permit habeas review of a range of legal and constitutional questions arising in immigration cases, reading Congress's new language only to limit judicial review of basic facts. Relying on *Nishimura Ekiu*, the Supreme Court proceeded to uphold habeas jurisdiction in a host of cases, including those of persons seeking to enter the country as well as other would-be immigrants who had been seized by authorities after entering the United States.

In 1961, Congress amended the immigration laws to set forth specific avenues of judicial review for immigration cases. Exclusion cases (those precluding entry) remained the province of habeas review, while deportation cases were to be reviewed in an appellate posture by the federal courts of appeals. Congress amended this scheme anew in two 1996 statutes, AEDPA and the Illegal Immigration Reform and Immigrant Responsibility Act, or IIRIRA. Together, these provisions merged deportation and exclusion cases into "removal" proceedings and purported to limit, or in some cases preclude altogether, judicial review of decisions made by immigration officers in such proceedings.

Several Supreme Court cases followed. In 2001, the court decided *INS v. St. Cyr*, involving Enrico St. Cyr, a Haitian citizen who had been admitted to the United States as a lawful permanent resident in 1986. St. Cyr pleaded guilty to selling drugs in 1996, a conviction that rendered him eligible to be removed from the United States. After failing to convince an immigration judge that he should receive a discretionary waiver of deportation, St. Cyr filed a habeas petition rearguing the point. At the Supreme Court, his case raised two questions. First, had IIRIRA withdrawn entirely the attorney general's preexisting discretionary authority to waive deportation of aliens convicted of certain crimes? Second, could the court even answer the first question in light of a provision in AEDPA purporting to "Eliminat[e] Custody Review by Habeas Corpus" and another provision in IIRIRA stating that "notwithstanding any other provision of law, no court shall have jurisdiction to review any final order of removal against an alien who is removable by reason of having committed [certain specified] criminal offense[s]"?

Writing for five justices, Justice Stevens held that notwithstanding these provisions, the federal courts retained habeas jurisdiction under 28 U.S.C. § 2241 to review "pure questions of law," such as whether IIRIRA withdrew the attorney general's discretion to waive deportation. This conclusion followed, in the majority's view, from "the longstanding rule requiring a clear statement of congressional intent to repeal habeas jurisdiction" and the strong presumption favoring judicial review of administrative actions. Continuing, Justice Stevens observed that interpreting the relevant provisions to preclude judicial review of legal issues here "would give rise to substantial constitutional questions." This followed, he wrote, because under the Suspension Clause, "some 'judicial intervention in deportation cases' is unquestionably 'required by the Constitution.'"

Only days on the heels of *St. Cyr*, the court decided *Zadvydas v. Davis*, again by a 5–4 margin. In an opinion by Justice Stephen Breyer, the majority reaffirmed that IIRIRA did not displace § 2241 habeas jurisdiction, this time in a case challenging the indefinite detention by the attorney general of an alien who had been ordered deported. Going further, the court held that the relevant postremoval detention statute, "read in light of the Constitution's demands...does not permit indefinite detention." Instead, the majority held, the statute was better read to "contain an implicit 'reasonable time' limitation, the application of which is subject to federal court review." Neither *St. Cyr* nor *Zadvydas* purported to be constitutional decisions, but both were heavily influenced by the idea that the Suspension Clause likely compelled their outcomes.

Neither decision, however, spoke to what the Constitution might require with respect to those seeking entry to the United States, including persons seeking asylum. Commentators and jurists have long debated whether earlier cases, including *Nishimura Ekiu* in particular, were driven by constitutional concerns as opposed to pure statutory interpretation. The latest chapter in these debates came in the court's 2020 decision in *Department of Homeland Security v. Thuraissigiam*. But before turning to *Thuraissigiam*, another body of habeas jurisprudence warrants discussion.

Terrorism

The story of how the privilege has confronted terrorism begins with developments in the United Kingdom. In 1971, facing the rise of Irish Republican Army and Loyalist violence over the status of Northern Ireland, the British government declared a state of emergency. The government initially invoked emergency powers from the original laws that governed the partition of Ireland in 1922. Soon, however, Parliament went further and took up amending the core terms of the English Habeas Corpus Act. In the Courts Act of 1971, Parliament repealed the original seventh section of the Habeas Corpus Act and in its place adopted legislation authorizing the temporary preventive detention of suspected terrorists—a category expressly inclusive of both British citizens and aliens. Parliament designed these changes, unlike the temporary defense acts passed during the world wars, to be permanent.

Under this framework, British law now permits the preventive or investigative detention of suspected terrorists for up to fourteen days. (A similar framework governs in Australia.) The governing statutory scheme affords persons detained on this basis multiple opportunities for judicial review as well as the opportunity to consult with and be represented by counsel. To combat terrorism and exclude terrorists from re-entry to the United Kingdom, Parliament also has authorized various other preventive and investigative measures, including, among other things, control orders that limit an individual's freedom of movement.

In the United States, the terrorist attacks of September 11, 2001, similarly ushered in a reconsideration of the habeas privilege and a retreat from the core protections of the English Habeas Corpus Act. Important developments in this regard began in the United States when, in 1950, the US Congress passed the Emergency Detention Act, which was a product of Cold War and McCarthy-era anticommunism politics. The act authorized the president to declare unilaterally an "Internal Security Emergency," after which he could arrest and detain individuals—including citizens—based solely on suspicion of likelihood of future engagement in spying or sabotage on behalf of enemies of the United States. In the act, Congress expressly declared that it was not suspending habeas corpus. (Members of Congress apparently believed that such a step was unnecessary, perhaps in reliance on the historical precedent of the mass detention of Japanese Americans during World War II.) Although the Emergency Detention Act provoked substantial academic criticism, members of Congress overwhelmingly supported the legislation. But President Truman did not. He vetoed the bill and called it a "mockery of the Bill of Rights" and a "long step toward totalitarianism." Truman also argued that "the provisions in [the act] would very probably prove ineffective to achieve the objective sought, since they would not suspend the writ of habeas corpus, and under our legal system to detain a man not charged with a crime would raise serious constitutional questions unless the writ of habeas corpus were suspended." Truman had history on his side, but both houses of Congress overrode his veto within a day.

In 1971, however, the US Congress changed course. That year, it repealed the Emergency Detention Act, no president having ever invoked its provisions. In its place, Congress adopted the Non-Detention Act, which provided that "no citizen shall be imprisoned or otherwise detained by the United States except pursuant to an Act of Congress." A major push for the law's passage came from the Japanese American Citizens League, which had launched a nationwide effort to repeal the Emergency Detention Act with the hope of preventing history from repeating itself.

Then came September 11, 2001. On that day, terrorists affiliated with al-Qaeda hijacked four commercial airliners. The hijackers flew two planes into Manhattan's World Trade Center towers, causing their collapse. They crashed a third plane into the Pentagon just across the river from Washington, DC. A fourth plane crashed in a Pennsylvania field after its crew and passengers fought back against their hijackers. Together, the attacks claimed almost three thousand lives.

Within days, the US Congress enacted the 2001 Authorization for Use of Military Force (AUMF). The AUMF empowered the president to "use all necessary and appropriate force against those nations, organizations, or persons he determines planned, authorized, committed, or aided the terrorist attacks that occurred on September 11, 2001 ... in order to prevent any future acts of international terrorism against the United States by such nations, organizations, or persons."

In carrying out the mandate of the AUMF, the American executive has pursued a lengthy and evolving war on terrorism. In prosecuting the war on many fronts, the US military has taken numerous suspected terrorists and others believed to possess ties to al-Qaeda and other terrorist organizations into custody. Those captured have included US citizens. In the case of John Walker Lindh, a citizen captured fighting with the Taliban in Afghanistan, the government prosecuted him criminally in due course. By contrast, in the cases of José Padilla and Yaser Hamdi, two US citizens taken into custody in 2002, the government labeled them "enemy combatants" and detained them without criminal charges. The US government acted similarly with respect to hundreds of other persons captured overseas in the war on terrorism who held no prior ties to the country. Also labeling those detainees enemy combatants, the government imprisoned them at the US naval base at Guantanamo Bay, Cuba.

Three major habeas cases arising out of these events made their way to the Supreme Court of the United States. The first was Padilla's. The government arrested Padilla in 2002 upon his arrival at Chicago's O'Hare International Airport, to which he had traveled, via Europe, from Pakistan. The government initially detained Padilla on a material witness warrant stemming from the ongoing grand jury investigation based in New York into the attacks of September 11. Approximately one month later, President George W. Bush issued an order declaring Padilla to be an enemy combatant. In his order, the president wrote that he had determined that Padilla was "closely associated with al Qaeda, an international terrorist organization with which the United States is at war"; had carried out "war-like acts, including conduct in preparation for acts of international terrorism" against the United States; "possesse[d] intelligence" that might assist the government in its counterterrorism efforts; and "represent[ed] a continuing, present and grave danger to the national security of the United States." The president further declared that Padilla's immediate detention was "necessary to prevent him from aiding al Qaeda in its efforts to attack the United States."

Through counsel, Padilla filed a habeas petition challenging his detention by the military as unconstitutional. His case, *Rumsfeld v. Padilla*, made it to the Supreme Court in 2004, only to be dismissed by a five-justice majority on the basis that he had filed his habeas petition in the wrong federal district. The fact that the government had moved Padilla to South Carolina in the days before he had filed his petition in New York doomed his efforts.

Four justices dissented, arguing that the court could and should reach the merits of Padilla's claims. As Justice Stevens viewed things, "At stake in this case is nothing less than the essence of a free society. Even more important than the method of selecting the people's rulers and their successors is the character of the constraints imposed on the Executive by the rule of law. Unconstrained executive detention for the purpose of investigating and preventing subversive activity is the hallmark of the Star Chamber." Justice Stevens also took issue with the government's detention of Padilla incommunicado without access to counsel.

As a result of the majority's opinion, Padilla remained in military custody and had to commence his habeas petition anew in the proper jurisdiction, which he did. When his case returned to the Supreme Court on a petition for certiorari, or review, the government requested permission to transfer him to civilian custody to commence criminal proceedings against him. The Supreme Court permitted the government to transfer Padilla and his habeas case became essentially moot because he no longer remained in military custody. All told, the military had detained Padilla without criminal charges for over three years before the government filed charges against him. Along the way, Padilla had protested consistently—but ultimately unsuccessfully—that his detention violated the Suspension Clause.

Unlike Padilla's case, the second major habeas case arising out of the war on terror to reach the Supreme Court in 2004 did lead to a decision on the merits. But that case, *Hamdi v. Rumsfeld*, did not result in an opinion that spoke for the court, as no opinion commanded five votes. The relevant facts stemmed from the 2001 capture in Afghanistan of Yaser Hamdi by Afghan Northern Alliance fighters, allies of the US military in the fight to overthrow the Taliban. Hamdi had been born in the United States but had grown up in Saudi Arabia; what he was, or was not, doing in Afghanistan comprised one of the contested aspects of his subsequent habeas case. In turning Hamdi over to the US military, the Northern Alliance reported that it had captured him fighting with the enemy Taliban. The US military first detained Hamdi at the naval base at Guantanamo Bay, Cuba. When it learned that Hamdi was a US citizen, it transferred him to a naval brig in South Carolina. There, the government labeled Hamdi an enemy combatant and claimed the power to detain him indefinitely for the duration of the war on terrorism.

On behalf of his son, Hamdi's father filed a habeas petition challenging Hamdi's detention. When the case eventually made its way to the Supreme Court, Hamdi's lawyers argued that as a citizen, he could not be detained outside the criminal process in the absence of a suspension. In response, the government argued that Congress had authorized Hamdi's detention in the AUMF and that Hamdi was not entitled to independent review of his classification or detention as an enemy combatant.

A fractured Supreme Court rejected the government's assertion that the executive could detain a citizen in this posture without some opportunity to challenge his classification as an enemy combatant. At the same time, the court held that nothing in the Suspension Clause precluded the government from detaining a citizen as an enemy combatant in the absence of a suspension. On this point, writing for a plurality of four justices but ultimately speaking for the court in delivering its judgment, Justice Sandra

Day O'Connor concluded that "there is no bar to this Nation's holding one of its own citizens as an enemy combatant."

Joined by Chief Justice William Rehnquist, Justice Anthony Kennedy, and Justice Breyer, Justice O'Connor resolved that the AUMF authorized the detention of all persons captured as part of the war on terrorism, whether citizens or not. Thus, she rejected the argument that the Non-Detention Act barred Hamdi's detention as a matter of federal statutory law. Four other justices disagreed. The plurality's holding controlled because Justice Clarence Thomas wrote separately to opine that he believed the executive possessed broad discretion to detain under the AUMF. In his view, Hamdi's detention fell "squarely within the Federal Government's war powers, and [the court] lack[ed] the expertise and capacity to second-guess that decision."

Justice O'Connor's opinion also rejected Hamdi's argument that his detention violated the Suspension Clause. It was of no moment that Congress had declined to suspend the privilege in the wake of September 11, 2001. (In *Hamdi*, the government's lawyers did not argue that the AUMF constituted a suspension.) In reaching this conclusion, Justice O'Connor emphasized the "context" of Hamdi's arrest, which involved "a United States citizen captured in a foreign combat zone." Likewise, Justice O'Connor's opinion relied heavily on the Supreme Court's 1942 World War II opinion in Ex parte *Quirin* for the proposition that, during wartime, the government can exercise its rights under the international laws of war, even with respect to US citizens.

Quirin had involved a group of German soldiers, or "saboteurs," who had landed on US shores with plans to engage in various acts of sabotage. Pursuant to a directive issued by President Roosevelt, the government charged the group with violations of the law of war and tried them before a military tribunal in a room at the US Department of Justice in Washington, DC. Notably, one of the saboteurs claimed and never renounced US citizenship.

The Supreme Court decided *Quirin* on an expedited basis—indeed, the court agreed to hear and decided the case in a matter of days. The relevant aspect of the *Quirin* holding for purposes of *Hamdi* stemmed from the *Quirin* court's conclusion that nothing in the Constitution precluded the government from trying an individual claiming US citizenship before a military commission for violations of the laws of war. Thus, in upholding the military trials in *Quirin*, the Supreme Court did not distinguish between the citizen and his fellow German saboteurs. This proved an important foundation for Justice O'Connor's opinion in *Hamdi*, which quoted *Quirin* for the proposition that "citizens who associate themselves with the military arm of the enemy government, and with its aid, guidance and direction enter this country bent on hostile acts, are enemy belligerents within the meaning of … the law of war." It followed, in her view, that the power to try and sentence a citizen during wartime under the law of war led inexorably to the conclusion that citizens also may be held as the equivalent of prisoners of war, a category recognized under the law of war, for the duration of hostilities.

But, the plurality concluded, the government did not enjoy unfettered discretion to detain someone like Hamdi. This is because, as Justice O'Connor wrote, "detention without trial 'is the carefully limited exception'" in the American constitutional tradition. This meant that the court should "not give short shrift to the values that this country holds dear or to the privilege that is American citizenship." Accordingly, her opinion declared that Hamdi must be given "a meaningful opportunity to contest the factual basis" for his classification "before a neutral decisionmaker." Such a hearing, she wrote, should "balanc[e] [the] serious competing interests" at stake—specifically, the individual liberty interests and the government's interest in preventing persons captured in wartime from returning to the battlefield. Justice O'Connor derived this framework from the court's due process jurisprudence developed in cases involving the removal of government benefits. Finally, Justice O'Connor declined to rule out the possibility that the government could rely upon hearsay evidence in such a hearing or that proceedings could take place before a military tribunal.

To make a holding, the plurality picked up the votes of Justices David Souter and Ruth Bader Ginsburg. Once the dust settled, however, it is not entirely clear just how much of a holding there was. This is because the two justices who joined the plurality opinion stated in their own separate opinion, written by Justice Souter, that they had joined solely to "give practical effect to the conclusions of eight Members of the Court rejecting the Government's position." Adding further distance between their position and the plurality's, when the court released the opinions in *Hamdi*, Justice Souter declared in a bench statement that he and Justice Ginsburg believed that on the existing record, "the government is detaining Hamdi in violation of the law, and that if the government comes up with nothing further, Hamdi is entitled to be released." Further, Justice Souter stated that he and Justice Ginsburg had "not even reach[ed] a constitutional claim on Hamdi's behalf or decide[d] a constitutional issue."

Two dissenting justices did reach the constitutional issues at play in the case. Justice Antonin Scalia, joined by Justice Stevens, first began by contending that the Non-Detention Act barred the detention of Hamdi as a US citizen and had not been overridden by the AUMF. Going further, the dissent concluded that Hamdi's detention violated the Suspension Clause. As Justice Scalia viewed things, the entire purpose of the clause, born out of English legal tradition, was to require that, absent suspension, "citizens aiding the enemy [be] treated as traitors subject to the criminal process." As Justice Scalia explained, "Where the Government accuses a citizen of waging war against it, our constitutional tradition has been to prosecute him in federal court for treason or some other crime. Where the exigencies of war prevent that, the Constitution's Suspension Clause, Art. I, § 9, cl. 2, allows Congress to relax the usual protections temporarily. Absent suspension, however, the

Executive's assertion of military exigency has not been thought sufficient to permit detention without charge." Maintaining that due process traditionally married with this idea, the dissent posited that "when a citizen was deprived of liberty because of alleged criminal conduct, those procedures typically required committal by a magistrate followed by indictment and trial."

Justice Scalia's dissent relied on extensive historical evidence, spanning from the origins of the English Habeas Corpus Act of 1679 through American history up to and through the Civil War. Thus, among other things, he pointed to the role of treason in the Anglo-American legal tradition and Blackstone's *Commentaries* on which Alexander Hamilton had relied in his discussion of the Suspension Clause in *Federalist* No. 84, when Hamilton quoted Blackstone for the proposition that "it is unreasonable to send a prisoner, and not to signify the crimes alleged against him." Justice Scalia also cited the purpose behind the suspensions directed at the Jacobites, Shays's Rebellion, the Burr conspiracy, the Civil War, and Reconstruction. Finally, he pointed to the government's treatment of prisoners during the War of 1812 as well as the writings of Thomas Jefferson and Justice Story.

The dissent further argued that Ex parte *Quirin* should not be read to support the plurality's position. On the contrary, Justice Scalia argued, the Civil War decision in Ex parte *Milligan* was better authority, both because of its proximity to the founding, which made it a stronger "indicator of original meaning," and because *Quirin* had been decided on a rushed basis. (*Quirin*, in the dissent's view, represented "not this Court's finest hour.") Justice Scalia maintained that *Milligan*'s holding that a citizen could not be tried by a military tribunal for violations of the law of war "where the courts are open and their process unobstructed" was more in keeping with "the Founders' general mistrust of military power permanently at the Executive's disposal." In *Quirin*, moreover, "it was uncontested that the prisoners were members of enemy forces" or "admitted enemy invaders." For these reasons, the dissent argued, *Quirin* should be limited to its "conceded facts."

The dissent concluded: "If the Suspension Clause does not guarantee the citizen that he will either be tried or released [in the absence of a suspension]...; if it merely guarantees the citizen that he will not be detained unless Congress by ordinary legislation says he can be detained; it guarantees him very little indeed." On this view, the Suspension Clause required Hamdi's release—not more process, and certainly not process that was the product of judicial balancing or, in a classic turn of phrase coined by Justice Scalia, the product of the plurality's "Mr. Fix-it Mentality." Thus, in the dissent's view, the government had two—and only two—options for lawfully detaining Hamdi: either initiate criminal proceedings against him or suspend the privilege to legalize his detention outside the criminal process.

In the wake of *Hamdi*, prominent legal scholars applauded the plurality's pragmatic balancing approach as offering more process than Hamdi would have enjoyed during a suspension. But it is far from obvious that Congress would have pursued a suspension had a court ordered Hamdi's discharge. It is also not entirely clear whether a suspension could have encompassed Hamdi because it is debatable whether Congress or the court would have determined that the required justifications for a suspension—namely, a "Rebellion or Invasion"—encompass overseas wars.

Either way, the decision marked a major turning point in habeas jurisprudence. To begin, there is tension between the *Hamdi* plurality's envisioned judicial balancing and how the suspension framework had long operated in Anglo-American practice. Historically, the relevant balancing of the needs of national security against individual liberty in times of crisis had been left to the political branches to determine whether the security of the state and the conditions of the moment justified a suspension and its dramatic effects on individual liberty.

Further, the traditional suspension model had long been predicated upon the idea, grounded in English law as chronicled by Hale and Coke, that persons owing allegiance who "raise war against the king" are "not properly enemies but rebels or traitors" and, as such, "they shall be punished as Traytors." To reach such persons, suspensions historically targeted those deemed to owe allegiance who "levy war" against their government. In Hamdi's case, once the government transported him for detention to American soil, his plight came to resemble those British subjects who fought with the French for the Jacobite cause. So many years earlier, Lord Mansfield had written that once the suspected traitors in that context were brought to English soil for detention, they could claim their rights under the Habeas Corpus Act to force a trial or else be discharged. The same analogy may be drawn to American Rebels captured in battle during the Revolutionary War brought to English soil. To legalize their detention without trial, Parliament had suspended the protections of the Habeas Corpus Act. *Hamdi* is hard to reconcile with these historical precedents. It is perhaps better viewed as an outgrowth of the World War II mass detention of Japanese Americans, which had already established, at least as historic precedent, that the government could claim the power to detain citizens outside the criminal process during wartime in the absence of a suspension.

The Suspension Clause and Guantanamo Bay

Hamdi's reconceptualization of the constitutional privilege as a procedural remedy, and not a constraint on detention per se, set the stage for the court's third and final major habeas decision arising out of the war on terrorism, *Boumediene v. Bush*. Decided in 2008, *Boumediene* involved the question whether the noncitizen detainees held at the US military installation at Guantanamo Bay, Cuba, could claim a constitutional right to habeas review of their classification and detention by the US government as enemy combatants in the war on terrorism.

There is evidence suggesting that in deciding where to hold such prisoners, the Bush administration may have chosen Guantanamo Bay in part based on a belief that it would fall outside the habeas jurisdiction of the US federal courts. Either way, in 2004, the Supreme Court rejected that proposition in *Rasul v. Bush*, holding that the existing habeas statutes governing the jurisdiction of the federal courts empowered the courts to review habeas petitions filed by detainees held at Guantanamo Bay. The *Rasul* decision triggered not one, but two, legislative responses. Both purported to strip any and all federal court jurisdiction over such petitions. The second of these statutes, the Military Commissions Act of 2006 (MCA), set the stage for *Boumediene*.

Notwithstanding the MCA's aggressive jurisdiction-stripping language, the Supreme Court held, 5–4, in an opinion written by Justice Anthony M. Kennedy, that Guantanamo Bay detainees could lay claim to "the constitutional privilege of habeas corpus, a privilege not to be withdrawn except in conformance with the Suspension Clause." As such, the majority held, Congress could not strip the courts of jurisdiction to hear petitions brought by Guantanamo detainees challenging their designations as enemy combatants.

This conclusion followed for several reasons. First, the court held—tackling a question that it had never decided before—that the Suspension Clause promises an affirmative right to judicial review that Congress may not displace except through a valid suspension. Relying on a host of sources from the Constitution's ratification debates, the majority concluded that the American founding generation assumed that the availability of the privilege was implicitly guaranteed under the Suspension Clause. In the court's words, "the Clause...ensures that, except during periods of formal suspension, the Judiciary will have a time-tested device, the writ, to maintain the 'delicate balance of governance' that is itself the surest safeguard of liberty."

10. A sign marks the location of Camp Justice, the area encompassing the military commissions established on the US naval base at Guantanamo Bay, Cuba.

Considerable historical evidence supported this conclusion. During the ratification debates over the Constitution, for example, various speakers declared, among other things, that the habeas "privilege...is essential to freedom," seemingly assuming that the writ was guaranteed. To be sure, it is not clear that the founding

generation had fully thought through how the privilege would
secured in the new constitutional framework. The US
Constitution does not mandate the creation of lower federal court
and instead leaves the decision whether to "ordain and establish"
such courts to Congress. At the time of the Constitution's
ratification, state courts were well established and possessed a
wealth of experience with habeas jurisdiction. This background
suggests that the founding generation likely assumed that, at a
minimum, state courts would be available to habeas petitioners.
In all events, the First Congress established inferior federal courts
and vested them with habeas jurisdiction in the Judiciary Act of
1789. It is that jurisdiction that had been displaced by the MCA.

Next, the court concluded that the detainees, who had no prior
association with the United States and were being confined
outside the formal territory of the United States, could claim the
protections of the US Constitution. The government had argued
that such persons "have no constitutional rights." Justice Kennedy
tackled the question by turning to "the history and origins of the
writ." Reviewing the relevant history, Justice Kennedy observed
that the founding generation constitutionalized the privilege
because "experience [had] taught...that the common-law writ all
too often had been insufficient to guard against the abuse of
monarchial power." He then traced the early origins of the writ
from its use as a means of "enforc[ing] the King's prerogative to
inquire into the authority of a jailer to hold a prisoner" through its
evolution into a judicial instrument wielded for restraining "the
King's power." Noting that the "writ remained an imperfect check"
during this period, Justice Kennedy explained that the English
Habeas Corpus Act of 1679 had "established procedures for
issuing the writ" and subsequently served as "the model upon
which the habeas statutes of the 13 American colonies
were based."

Justice Kennedy next addressed the specific question whether
"foreign nationals, apprehended and detained in distant countries

ıg a time of serious threats to our Nation's security, may assert
privilege of the writ and seek its protection." To do so, Justice
ennedy moved away from the English Habeas Corpus Act and
urned back to the common law writ. Asking what the common
law writ could do in 1789, he concluded that "at common law a
petitioner's status as an alien was not a categorical bar to habeas
corpus relief." Instead, he noted, common law courts had
"entertained habeas petitions brought by enemy aliens detained in
England...at least in the sense that the courts held hearings to
determine the threshold question of entitlement to the writ." To
the extent that courts during this period did not go any further in
cases involving prisoners of war, Justice Kennedy argued, "there
was greater justification for doing so in the context of declared
wars with other nation states."

Turning to the question of geographic breadth of the common law
writ, the majority found a similarly complicated historical record.
For this reason, Justice Kennedy next addressed alternative
considerations. He first highlighted the "unique status of
Guantanamo Bay" and observed that "no law other than the laws
of the United States applies at the naval station." He next
referenced "the particular dangers of terrorism in the modern age"
and the lack of clear historical analogy between the war on
terrorism and the declared wars between nation-states that
England had confronted in the period leading up to the American
Revolutionary War.

It did not matter to the majority that the US government did not
exercise formal sovereignty over Guantanamo Bay. This is
because, Justice Kennedy wrote, "the obvious and uncontested
fact [is] that the United States, by virtue of its complete
jurisdiction and control over the base [under its perpetual lease
with the Cuban government], maintains de facto sovereignty over
this territory." This and other considerations led the majority to
discount the court's World War II decision in *Johnson v.
Eisentrager*, which had declined to award habeas relief to certain

German nationals who had been captured and tried for war crimes in China and later moved to Germany to serve their sentences. That case, the court concluded, presented distinguishing considerations, including the fact that in Germany, the United States lacked both de jure sovereignty and plenary control over Landsberg Prison, where the petitioners were detained. Also relevant to Justice Kennedy's analysis was the fact that the *Eisentrager* petitioners "did not contest, it seems, the Court's assertion that they were 'enemy alien[s].'" By contrast, these detainees disputed that they were enemy combatants.

From here, the majority relied on "objective factors and practical concerns, not formalism," to support its holding. In Justice Kennedy's view, "at least three factors are relevant in determining the reach of the Suspension Clause": the citizenship and status of the detainee and how that status determination was made; where apprehension and detention occurred; and "the practical obstacles inherent in resolving the prisoner's entitlement to the writ." Further, declining to apply the Suspension Clause to Guantanamo Bay would make it "possible for the political branches to govern [there] without legal constraint," a proposition that he rejected as at odds with American constitutional tradition. Justice Kennedy was also concerned that here, "the consequence of error may be detention of persons for the duration of hostilities that may last a generation or more." Declaring the "writ of habeas corpus...an indispensable mechanism for monitoring the separation of powers," it followed in the majority's view that the Suspension Clause should be given "full effect at Guantanamo Bay."

Finally, the court had to determine whether the limited procedures established by Congress in the MCA, which provided detainees the opportunity to contest their status before military commissions and a limited chance for appeal, provided constitutionally sufficient process. Concluding that those procedures fell short on many fronts, Justice Kennedy deemed the MCA "an unconstitutional suspension of the writ." It followed, in majority's view, that the detainees should be given a broader ... of procedures to challenge their status as enemy combatants in ...he federal courts. (The court said little about what such proceedings would entail, leaving the details and relevant procedures to be worked out by the lower federal courts.)

Two dissenting opinions followed, both speaking for the four in the minority. The first, authored by Chief Justice John Roberts, complained that the court had erroneously held "inadequate the most generous set of procedural protections ever afforded aliens detained by this country as enemy combatants." The chief justice also found fault with the fact that the *Hamdi* plurality had held that it would be constitutionally permissible in the case of a citizen to offer a hearing before a military tribunal, while here, the court provided that noncitizens should be permitted to have their hearings in the far more independent federal courts. In his view, "surely the Due Process Clause does not afford non-citizens in such circumstances greater protection than citizens are due." Predicting that the detainees would meet with little success in any event, Chief Justice Roberts complained that the "majesty [of the privilege] is hardly enhanced by its extension to a jurisdictionally quirky outpost, with no tangible benefit to anyone."

Justice Scalia also dissented. For him, "the writ as preserved in the Constitution could not possibly extend farther than the common law provided when the [Suspension] Clause was written." Because he interpreted the historical record to be quite clear that "the writ of habeas corpus does not, and never has, run in favor of aliens abroad," that was enough to dispose of the case. (This approach married with Justice Scalia's view of constitutional interpretation, known as originalism, which seeks to interpret the Constitution in keeping with how it was understood during the founding period.) Accordingly, Justice Scalia disputed the proposition that the writ followed the king's officers wherever they went, highlighting the geographic limitations of the English Habeas Corpus Act and the fact that it did not extend to all parts of the British Empire. Given that the Suspension Clause limits suspension "almost entirely to instances of domestic crisis," Justice Scalia read the clause to apply exclusively to domestic US soil and not to Guantanamo Bay, which he deemed to be "abroad."

Justice Scalia also argued that *Eisentrager* supported his position because there, the court had emphasized that in the face of any extension of "constitutional protections beyond the citizenry…, it was the alien's presence within its territorial jurisdiction that gave the Judiciary power to act." In all events, Justice Scalia believed that the plight of the detainees at Guantanamo Bay was comparable not to the *Eisentrager* criminal defendants, but instead to "the more than 400,000 prisoners of war detained in the United States alone during World War II." Of those, Justice Scalia observed, "not a single one was accorded the right to have his detention validated by a habeas corpus action in federal court—and that despite the fact that they were present on U.S. soil."

The adaptable common law writ

Together, *Boumediene* and *Hamdi* reconceptualized the American constitutional habeas privilege as a procedural mechanism—that is, as promising additional process to the prisoner rather than the possibility of outright release. Even Chief Justice Roberts's dissent in *Boumediene* characterized "habeas" as "most fundamentally a procedural right."

Thus, every member of the *Boumediene* court simply took it for granted that the government had the authority to detain persons at Guantanamo Bay as enemy combatants. The justices divided instead over what process the government needed to provide along the way. In this respect, *Hamdi* and *Boumediene* departed from the traditional suspension framework associated with the seventh section of the English Habeas Corpus Act, which offered a remedy of discharge to those who could claim the protection of domestic law when they were not tried in due course. (Of course, the existence of a suspension displaced this regime.) That framework, accordingly, looked backward to ask whether one had been *already* afforded process (specifically, a criminal trial); it was never about the promise of more process.

Boumediene also differed from *Hamdi* in important respects. Justice Scalia's *Boumediene* dissent correctly noted that the decision was the first of its kind to apply the Suspension Clause to persons lacking prior association with the United States who were also being detained on what is, formally speaking, foreign soil. In the seventeenth and eighteenth centuries, habeas proceedings sorted those who could invoke the protections of the Habeas Corpus Act from those who could not, with allegiance serving as a critical factor in the analysis. As the movement of prisoners during the Revolutionary War reveals, geography mattered too, given that the Habeas Corpus Act did not apply throughout the British Empire. Allegiance and geography, however, played at most a limited role in the majority's *Boumediene* analysis. This being said, concerns over geography may explain why the majority emphasized Guantanamo Bay's "unique status" that rendered it more like a US territory than an overseas military outpost. In all events, some commentators view *Boumediene* as having expanded the reach of the writ as a matter of American constitutional law.

Boumediene did so by embracing a common law vision of habeas corpus. In Anglo-American law, the judicially created common law writ has long been celebrated for its adaptability and potential to evolve. *Somerset v. Stewart* and the American fugitive slave cases stand as examples of that potential and its significance. Historians have also documented how the common law writ often reached further than the Habeas Corpus Act to be wielded by judges throughout the British Empire.

This adaptability helped the *Boumediene* majority confront what it viewed as novel questions raised by the war on terrorism, which the court contrasted with "declared wars with other nation states." The court also was likely aware that the Bush administration publicly had taken the position that a good portion of the Geneva Conventions and international law did not apply to the Guantanamo detainees, something that had led many commentators to refer to Guantanamo Bay as a "legal black hole." These concerns are represented in Justice Kennedy's opinion, which emphasized that if the court sided with the government in the case, "the political branches" would be permitted "to govern without legal constraint" at the Guantanamo Bay base.

In embracing a common law model of habeas, the *Boumediene* majority expressly declined to follow an originalist approach and emphasized that "the Court has been careful not to foreclose the possibility that the protections of the Suspension Clause have expanded along with post-1789 developments that define the present scope of the writ." Because "common-law habeas corpus was, above all, an adaptable remedy" and "its precise application and scope changed depending upon the circumstances," the *Boumediene* court concluded that Suspension Clause jurisprudence should do the same.

Crossing the Atlantic to return to Great Britain, one finds a similar approach in the UK Supreme Court's 2017 decision in *Al-Waheed v. Ministry of Defence*. Relying in part on *Boumediene*, the lead opinion for the UK Supreme Court, delivered by Lord Jonathan Sumption, recognized that where, as is common in cases of suspected terrorists, there are "issue[s] about whether the applicant was in fact an enemy," habeas courts should exercise jurisdiction to review the petitioner's status. In so doing, Lord Sumption distinguished cases in which the status of prisoners of war and enemy aliens was not in dispute such that there existed a lesser need for judicial review. He also defended a broad vision of habeas jurisdiction: "A writ of habeas corpus is a personal remedy directed against the person alleged to have possession or control of the applicant. Jurisdiction to issue it depends on the respondent being within the jurisdiction of the court, and not on the location of the applicant. There is no principle to the effect that the writ is not available where the applicant has been captured in the course of armed conflict, if he disputes the status which is said to make his detention lawful or otherwise challenges its lawfulness." Thus, the opinion concluded, one detained by British forces in Afghanistan as an alleged enemy combatant may challenge that detention in the British courts via habeas—even where, as in the case of Al-Waheed, the petitioner is a foreign (Iraqi) citizen detained on foreign soil.

Al-Waheed stands as another example in the tradition of the common law writ, an evolving institution that has long witnessed judges play a crucial role in protecting individual liberty. An important question in the early twenty-first century is whether this common law vision of habeas can coexist with the privilege that was long associated with the seventh section of the English Habeas Corpus Act of 1679 such that the two visions of habeas can work toward that same end. Great Britain has retreated from the act's framework, which was always a possibility, given that the act constituted parliamentary legislation subject to repeal at any time. But in the United States, the founding generation constitutionalized the privilege associated with the English Habeas Corpus Act in the Suspension Clause, intending for those protections to endure. *Hamdi* walks back from that understanding, sanctioning as it does the idea that the government may detain someone who may claim the protection of domestic law outside the criminal process in the absence of a valid suspension.

The law in the United States and the United Kingdom has therefore landed in a similar place insofar as both permit the detention of citizens for national security purposes outside the criminal process and in the absence of a suspension. Notably, however, under *Hamdi*, US citizens detained as enemy combatants enjoy fewer legal protections than their British counterparts. This is because the United Kingdom strictly limits national security detentions in duration to fourteen days and subjects them to regular judicial review. The plurality in *Hamdi*, meanwhile, concluded that citizen enemy combatants potentially may be held for the duration of the war on terrorism—however long that may be—so long as a tribunal holds at the outset that sufficient evidence supports the government's initial determination that an individual may be a terrorist. Some might view *Hamdi*, accordingly, as an example of the pitfalls of an adaptable writ—that is, it shows that what can be expanded can also be retracted in turn.

On the heels of *Hamdi* and *Boumediene*, the latest chapter in US Suspension Clause jurisprudence is the 2020 Supreme Court decision in *Department of Homeland Security v. Thuraissigiam*, which muddies the waters even more. Vijayakumar Thuraissigiam, a Sri Lankan national, entered the United States clandestinely and was apprehended by a Border Patrol agent within twenty-five yards of the border. Once in government custody, he sought asylum in administrative proceedings, but he failed to convince immigration officials that he had a "credible fear of persecution" upon return to his native country. Had he succeeded in demonstrating a credible fear, Thuraissigiam would have been spared so-called expedited removal as provided for under IIRIRA, and afforded additional procedural opportunities to seek asylum in the United States. Notwithstanding a provision in IIRIRA that restricts judicial review of "the determination" by immigration officials that an applicant lacks a credible fear of persecution, Thuraissigiam sought a writ of habeas corpus in federal court, contending that he satisfied the credible fear test while also challenging the fairness of the proceedings. In his petition, Thuraissigiam argued that under both the Suspension Clause and the Due Process Clause, he was entitled to a new and more extensive hearing. Thuraissigiam also sought entry to the United States.

Joined by Chief Justice Roberts and Justices Thomas, Neil Gorsuch, and Brett Kavanaugh, Justice Samuel Alito wrote for the court and rejected Thuraissigiam's arguments across the board. Although no immigration laws existed either in the United States or in Great Britain during the founding period, Justice Alito posited that the relevant inquiry should ask how the founding generation understood the Suspension Clause in 1789. Thuraissigiam's claim failed because, in Justice Alito's view, habeas during that period was "a means to secure release from unlawful detention" and did not extend to an invocation of the writ "to achieve an entirely different end, namely, to obtain additional administrative review of his asylum claim and ultimately to obtain authorization to stay in this country." Nothing in *St. Cyr* counseled otherwise. That case was distinguishable in Justice Alito's view because it applied to "aliens already in the country who were held in custody pending deportation," as opposed to those seeking entry. Nor did *Boumediene* help Thuraissigiam, because it involved petitioners who "sought only to be released from Guantanamo, not to enter th[e] country." For good measure, Justice Alito's opinion also rejected the idea that *Somerset v. Stewart* helped Thuraissigiam. This was because, in that case, Lord Mansfield ordered Somerset's release, something that "fell within the historic core of habeas."

As for Thuraissigiam's due process argument, Justice Alito noted that "while aliens who have established connections in this country have due process rights in deportation proceedings, the Court long ago held that Congress is entitled to set the conditions for an alien's lawful entry into this country and that, as a result, an alien at the threshold of initial entry cannot claim any greater rights under the Due Process Clause." It did not matter that Thuraissigiam was taken into custody on US soil because Congress possesses "plenary authority to decide which aliens to admit" to the country. Further, the majority emphasized that the court's precedents provide that even aliens paroled in the country while pending removal are treated for due process purposes as if they had been stopped at the border. It followed, in Justice Alito's view, that an asylum seeker like Thuraissigiam had "no entitlement to procedural rights other than those afforded by statute."

Justices Breyer and Ginsburg concurred in the judgment, albeit narrowly. In their view, the statutory scheme was constitutional as applied to Thuraissigiam, but they would go no further. As Justice Breyer understood Thuraissigiam's arguments, they asked "that the habeas court make indeterminate and highly record-intensive judgments on matters of degree." But, he concluded, there existed no precedent "suggesting that the Suspension Clause demands parsing procedural compliance at so granular a level."

Justice Sonia Sotomayor, joined by Justice Elena Kagan, dissented. She contended that in countless habeas cases following in the wake of *Nishimura Ekiu*, the court had heard "claims indistinguishable from those" raised by Thuraissigiam, which, in her view, encompassed both mixed questions of law and fact and legal challenges to "procedural defects" in the removal procedures that Congress had prescribed. Justice Sotomayor argued, moreover, that *Nishimura Ekiu* should be read as a Suspension Clause decision, a proposition that the majority rejected. She also relied on fugitive slave cases as support for the proposition that common law courts in habeas granted release to such petitioners "to enter Territories not considered their own, and thus ordered the kind of release that the Court claims falls outside the purview of the common-law writ." Finally, Justice Sotomayor's dissent worried that "taken to its extreme, a rule conditioning due process rights on lawful entry would permit Congress to constitutionally eliminate all procedural protections for any noncitizen the Government deems unlawfully admitted and summarily deport them no matter how many decades they have lived here."

Thuraissigiam highlights that the debate wages on over the proper role of the habeas privilege in American constitutional law.

Justice Alito correctly noted that the classic remedy associated with the English Habeas Corpus Act was discharge, but *Hamdi* and *Boumediene*, grounded in a common law vision of habeas, had held that habeas petitioners could invoke the Suspension Clause to secure additional process—precisely what Thuraissigiam sought in his petition. *Boumediene*, moreover, celebrated the writ's potential to expand and evolve to confront modern circumstances. *Thuraissigiam* appears to walk back those holdings. Further, when paired with another 2020 Supreme Court decision, *Agency for International Development v. Alliance for Open Society International, Inc.*, *Thuraissigiam* also appears to renew emphasis on geography as a limiting factor in determining the sweep of the US Constitution. (In that case, a 5–4 majority opinion written by Justice Kavanaugh posited that "it is long settled as a matter of American constitutional law that foreign citizens outside U.S. territory do not possess rights under the U.S. Constitution.")

Like *Hamdi* and *Boumediene* before it, *Thuraissigiam* raises the question whether the American constitutional habeas privilege can embrace a role grounded in the English Habeas Corpus Act that imposes substantive constraints on executive detention and at the same time encompass a privilege derived from a common law model of habeas like that employed in *Boumediene* and *Al-Waheed* that can evolve over time. It is not at all clear why the constitutional habeas privilege cannot do both, especially if one conceives of the common law writ as providing due process, which is guaranteed by the US Constitution and an outgrowth of the promise made in Chapter 39 of the original Magna Carta that "No free man shall be taken or imprisoned . . . except by the legal judgment of his peers or by the law of the land." To this end, one possible approach going forward would associate the common law writ of habeas corpus within modern due process jurisprudence (on which, it bears noting, the *Hamdi* plurality relied), while leaving the Suspension Clause to enforce the core protections of the English Habeas Corpus Act that so strongly influenced its ratification. Either way, one of the greatest challenges for American habeas jurisprudence will be to confront the question whether there is a way for a habeas writ grounded in the US Constitution to fulfill both of these roles going forward. More generally, in charting the writ's future, courts everywhere will be called on to honor the privilege's historical role as "essential to freedom" while ensuring that habeas plays a meaningful role in a much-changed world.

Conclusion

The writ of habeas corpus has long enjoyed celebrated status as a palladium of liberty. There is much in the historical record that supports placing the storied writ on such a pedestal. Thus, the writ of habeas corpus has served as a vehicle for securing the freedom of political prisoners and even slaves. Habeas jurisdiction also has provided a forum for the declaration of bedrock constitutional rights in criminal cases. But it is also the case that habeas corpus has sometimes fallen short of deserving recognition as a guardian of Anglo-American freedom. Indeed, as the World War II mass incarceration of Japanese Americans reveals, habeas is sometimes only as effective as the politics of the time permit.

Much of this story told here is part of the broader debate over how the rule of law confronts emergencies. One view, represented by the US Supreme Court's decision in Ex parte *Milligan* just after the Civil War, instructs that "the Constitution of the United States is a law for rulers and people, equally in war and in peace." Lord Atkin's dissent from the British Law Lords' decision during World War II in *Liversidge v. Anderson* echoed this idea, positing that "the laws...speak the same language in war as in peace." The other view, and one that has increasingly controlled in times of war and threats to the national order, argues that the law must balance individual liberties against the pressing needs of the politics of the moment. Consider, in this regard, *Liversidge*, which upheld the internment of British citizens during World War II, and *Hamdi v. Rumsfeld*, which upheld the military detention of American citizens during the war on terrorism. (It did not matter in either case that the relevant legislature had declined to suspend habeas.)

It is not obvious that the law must settle at such a point of repose. Many see these kinds of decisions as out of keeping with the core ideals at the heart of a constitutional democracy. Consider the words of former Israeli Supreme Court President Aharon Barak: "This is the destiny of a democracy—it does not see all means as acceptable, and the ways of its enemies are not always open before it. A democracy must sometimes fight with one hand tied behind its back. Even so, a democracy has the upper hand. The rule of law and the liberty of an individual constitute important components in its understanding of security. At the end of the day, they strengthen its spirit and this strength allows it to overcome its difficulties."

The history of habeas corpus reveals what the law *can* achieve, not necessarily what it always *has* achieved. In some respects, modern habeas law in both Great Britain and the United States has retreated, turning away as it has from the core protections of the English Habeas Corpus Act that for so long were at the heart of the story of the privilege. At the same time, Anglo-American habeas jurisprudence has expanded the writ in other ways. Thus, the writ has evolved to carry out new roles, as, for example, it has done in slavery, criminal, and immigration cases. Likewise, the writ has evolved to reach new places, including Guantanamo Bay, Cuba, and Afghanistan. Finally, the writ has evolved to reach new categories of persons, including noncitizens captured overseas as part of the war on terrorism.

The great challenge for Anglo-American habeas jurisprudence going forward—and particularly in the United States, where a habeas privilege is constitutionalized—will be to ensure that as the writ expands in its role and reach, it also continues to fulfill its historic office as a tool for promoting liberty and dramatically limiting the power of the executive to deprive individuals of their freedom, even in times of war. More generally, wherever the storied writ of habeas corpus constitutes part of the legal canon, it will continue to confront many of the formidable challenges of the times. These include the blurring of geographic boundaries that has come with globalization, expanding migration, problems that undermine the criminal justice system, including systemic racism, and wars that do not fit into the classical model around which much international and domestic law was developed. In so doing, jurists would do well to recall the period when the writ of habeas corpus earned Blackstone's praise as a "second *magna carta*," for that history tells a story of a habeas writ that could bring even the king of England to his knees before the law. It is a writ, in other words, with endless possibilities.

References

Introduction

1 William Blackstone, *The Oxford Edition of Blackstone's Commentaries on the Laws of England*, ed. Ruth Paley (Oxford: Oxford University Press, 2016), *126, *131, *133.

Lettre Adressée aux Habitants de la Province de Quebec, October 26, 1774, in *Journals of the Continental Congress, 1774–1789*, ed. Worthington Chauncey Ford, vol. 1 (Washington, DC: Government Printing Office, 1904), 88, 107–8.

Alexander Hamilton, "The Federalist No. 84," in *The Federalist Papers*, ed. Clinton Rossiter (New York: Signet Classic, New American Library, 2003), 511.

Statement of Judge Increase Sumner, Debates in the Convention of the Commonwealth of Massachusetts, on the Adoption of the Federal Constitution, January 26, 1788, in *The Debates in the Several State Conventions on the Adoption of the Federal Constitution, as Recommended by the General Convention at Philadelphia, in 1787*, ed. Jonathan Elliot, vol. 2, 2nd ed. (Philadelphia: J. B. Lippincott, 1891), 109.

Great Charter of Liberties, ch. 39 (1215), in *Select Documents of English Constitutional History*, ed. George Burton Adams and H. Morse Stephens (New York: Macmillan, 1904), 42, 47.

Sir Edward Coke, *The Second Part of the Institutes of the Laws of England* (1628; London: E & R Brooke, 1797), 54.

Codd v. Turback, (1615) 3 Bulstrode 109–110, 81 Eng. Rep. 94 (K.B.).

U.S. Const. art. I, § 9, cl. 2.

David Clark and Gerrard McCoy, *Habeas Corpus: Australia, New Zealand and the South Pacific* (Sydney, NSW: Federation Press, 2000).

Canadian Charter of Rights and Freedoms, Part I of the Constitution Act, 1982, *being* Schedule B to the Canada Act, 1982, c. 11 (U.K.).

India Const. art. 32, § 2; art. 226, § 1.

Constitution of Ireland 1937 art. 40, § 4.

Haim H. Cohn, "The First Fifty Years of the Supreme Court of Israel," *Journal of Supreme Court History* 24 (1999): 3.

Constitution of Barbados 1966, § 13.

Habeas Corpus Act, Act No. 8724, December 21, 2007 (S. Kor.).

S. Afr. Const., 1996 Ch. 2, § 35.

New Zealand Bill of Rights Act 1990, pt. 2, § 23.

European Convention on Human Rights art. 5, 213 U.N.T.S. 221, 226, November 4, 1950.

Vicki C. Jackson, "World Habeas Corpus," *Cornell Law Review* 91 (2006): 303.

Chapter 1

Amanda L. Tyler, "A 'Second Magna Carta': The English Habeas Corpus Act and the Statutory Origins of the Habeas Privilege," *Notre Dame Law Review* 91 (2016): 1949.

Douglass C. North and Barry R. Weingast, "Constitutions and Commitment: The Evolution of Institutions Governing Public Choice in Seventeenth-Century England," *Journal of Economic History* 49 (1989): 803, 808–24.

Darnel's Case, (1627) 3 Cobbett's St. Tr. 1 (Eng.).

J. A. Guy, "The Origins of the Petition of Right Reconsidered," *Journal of History* 25 (1982): 289, 289–94.

Paul D. Halliday, *Habeas Corpus: From England to Empire* (Cambridge, MA: Belknap Press of Harvard University Press, 2010), 1, 30, 48–53, 55–56, 65, 138–39, 156–60, 220–23, 226, 229–31, 234, 236–40, 392.

Mark Kishlansky, "Tyranny Denied: Charles I, Attorney General Heath, and the Five Knights' Case," *Journal of History* 42 (1999): 53, 63–64.

Remarks of Sir Edward Coke in Parliament, April 26, 1628, in *Commons Debates 1628*, ed. Robert C. Johnson and Mary Frear Keeler, vol. 3 (Rochester, NY: University of Rochester Press, 1977), 95.

David Chan Smith, *Sir Edward Coke and the Reformation of the Laws: Religion, Politics and Jurisprudence, 1578-1616* (Cambridge: Cambridge University Press, 2014), 270.

Roger Lockyer, *The Early Stuarts: A Political History of England 1603-1642* (New York: Longman, 1989), 336-45.

The Petition of Right, 1628, 3 Car. 1, c. 1 (Eng.).

Linda S. Popofsky, "Habeas Corpus and 'Liberty of the Subject': Legal Arguments for the Petition of Right in the Parliament of 1628," *Historian* 41 (1979): 257.

Elizabeth Read Foster, "Petitions and the Petition of Right," *Journal of British Studies* 14 (1974): 21, 27.

E. R. Adair and A. F. Pollard, "Historical Revisions: XIV—The Petition of Right," *History* (n.s.) 5 (1920): 99, 101.

Habeas Corpus Act, 1641, 16 Car. 1, c. 10 (Eng.).

Earl of Clarendon Case, (1667) 6 Cobbett's St. Tr. 317, 330-31 (Eng.).

1 Blackstone, *Commentaries*, *126, *131, *133.

Jenkes Case, (1676) 6 Cobbett's St. Tr. 1189, 1190, 1196, 1207 (Eng.).

Habeas Corpus Act, 1679, 31 Car. 2, c. 2 (Eng.), reprinted in *The Founders' Constitution*, ed. Philip B. Kurland and Ralph Lerner, vol. 3 (Chicago: University of Chicago Press, 1987), 310, 311.

3 Blackstone, *Commentaries*, *132-35, *137.

Coke, *The Second Part of the Institutes*, 54.

4 Blackstone, *Commentaries*, *432.

Henry Care, *English Liberties, or the Free-Born Subject's Inheritance* (London: G. Larkin for Benjamin Harris, 1680?), 129.

An Act for Preventing Wrongous Imprisonment, and against Undue Delays in Trials, Acts of the Parliament of Scotland, 1701 (Criminal Procedure Act of 1701), 12 Will. 3, c. 6 (Scot.).

An Act for Better Securing the Liberty of the Subject 1781, 21 & 22 Geo. 3, c. 11, § XVI (Ir.).

Chapter 2

Amanda L. Tyler, *Habeas Corpus in Wartime: From the Tower of London to Guantanamo Bay* (New York: Oxford University Press, 2017), 35-61.

W. B. Gray, "The Scottish Deportees of 1683 and the Habeas Corpus Act," *Juridical Review* 35 (1923): 353.

An Act to Attaint James Duke of Monmouth of High Treason 1685, 1 James II, c. 2 (Eng.).

House of Lords Journal 14 (1689) (Eng.), 135.

Debates of the House of Commons, from the Year 1667 to the Year 1694,
ed. Anchitell Grey. vol. 10 (London: D. Henry & R. Cave &
J. Emonson, 1763), 139–45.

Rex. v. Wyndham, (1723) 1 Strange 3 (K.B.).

Old Bailey Proceedings Supplementary Material, Ebenezer Smith
Platt, February 19, 1777, accessed February 1, 2020, http://www.
oldbaileyonline.org/browse.jsp?div=o17770219-1 (discussing
Wyndham's case).

John L. Roberts, *The Jacobite Wars: Scotland and the Military
Campaigns of 1714 and 1745* (Edinburgh: Polygon at Edinburgh,
2002), 35–37, 54–55, 175–88.

The King against the Earl of Orrery, Lord North and Grey, Bishop of
Rochester, Kelly, and Cockran, Prisoners in the Tower, (1722) 88
Eng. Rep. 75 (K.B.); 8 Mod. 96, 5th ed. (corrected 1795).

Halliday, *Habeas Corpus*, 32–35, 134–39, 146, 170–73, 212–58.

Amanda L. Tyler, "Suspension as an Emergency Power," *Yale Law
Journal* 118 (2009): 600, 614–22.

William Pickering, *An Old Story Re-told from the "Newcastle Courant":
The Rebellion of 1745* (Printed for private circulation, 1881),
196–211, 203–8.

Stuart Reid, *Culloden Moor 1746: The Death of the Jacobite Cause*
(Westport, CT: Praeger, 2005), 87, 88–90.

Rex. v. Townley, (1746) 18 Cobbett's St. Tr. 329, 348 (Eng.).

1 Blackstone, *Commentaries*, *361.

Treason Act, 1695, 7 & 8 Will. 3, c. 3 (Eng.).

U.S. Const. art. III, § 3, cl. 1.

7 & 8 Will. 3, c. 3.

John H. Langbein, *The Origins of Adversary Criminal Trial* (Oxford:
Oxford University Press, 2003), 67–105.

Henry Care, *English Liberties, or the Free-Born Subject's Inheritance*,
5th ed. (Boston: J. Franklin, 1721), 185.

Somerset v. Stewart, (1772) 98 Eng. Rep. 499 (K.B.), 1 Lofft 1.

William R. Cotter, "The Somerset Case and the Abolition of Slavery in
England," *History* 79, no. 255 (1994): 31.

An Act for the Abolition of the Slave Trade, 1807, 47 Geo. 3,
c. 36 (Eng.).

Slavery Abolition Act, 1833, 3 & 4 Will. 4, c. 73 (Eng.).

Chapter 3

Amanda L. Tyler, "Habeas Corpus and the American Revolution," *California Law Review* 103 (2015): 635.

Care, *English Liberties* (5th ed.), 185.

1 Blackstone, *Commentaries*, *133.

4 Blackstone, *Commentaries*, *286.

3 Blackstone, *Commentaries*, *137–*38.

"1774 Statement of Violation of Rights," in *Journals of the Continental Congress, 1774–1789*, ed. Worthington Chauncey Ford, vol. 1 (Washington, DC: Government Printing Office, 1904), 68.

Wilkes v. Wood, (1763) 98 Eng. Rep. 489 (K.B.).

"Observations upon the Charter of the Province of New-York (1684)," in *Documents Relative to the Colonial History of the State of New-York*, ed. John Romeyn Brodhead, vol. 3 (Albany, NY: Weed, Parsons, 1853), 357, 357.

David S. Lovejoy, "Equality and Empire: The New York Charter of Libertyes, 1683," *William & Mary Quarterly* 21 (1964): 493, 510–14.

Acts of the North Carolina General Assembly, 1749 23 (1905), 317.

"Order of the Privy Council of Great Britain Concerning Acts of the North Carolina General Assembly (April 8, 1754)," in *Colonial and State Records of North Carolina*, ed. William Laurence Saunders, vol. 5 (Raleigh, NC: Josephus Daniels, Printer to the States, 1887), 116.

Declaration of Independence, para. 22 (U.S. 1776).

24 Geo. III, c. 3 (Quebec), in *Observations on a Pamphlet, Entitled A State of the Present Form of Government of the Province of Quebec . . .* (London: J. Stockdale, 1790), 16, 33–47.

Halliday, *Habeas Corpus*, 259–316.

Lettre Adressée aux Habitants de la Province de Quebec, October 26, 1774, in *Journals of the Continental Congress, 1774–1789*, 1:68, 88, 107–8.

Letter from Lord George Germain to the Lords Commanders of the Admiralty, December 27, 1775, (Gr. Brit.) CO 5/122/398, National Archives.

The Annual Register, or a View of the History, Politics, and Literature, for the Year 1775, ed. J. Dodsley, vol. 18 (London: J. Dodsley, 1776), 187.

Letter from Lord Hugh Palliser to the Earl of Sandwich, December 29, 1775, in *The Private Papers of John, Earl of Sandwich, First Lord of the Admiralty 1771–1782*, ed. G. R. Barnes and J. H. Owen, vol. 1 (London: Navy Records Society, 1932), 87.

Ethan Allen, *A Narrative of Colonel Ethan Allen's Captivity, Written by Himself* (Burlington, VT: H. Johnson, 1838).

Remarks of Lord Frederick North given to the House of Commons on February 6, 1777, in William Cobbett, *The Parliamentary History of England: From the Earliest Period to the Year 1803*, ed. T. C. Hansard, vol. 19 (London: T. C. Hansard, 1814), 4.

An Act to Impower His Majesty to Secure and Detain Persons Charged with, or Suspected of, the Crime of High Treason, Committed in Any of His Majesty's Colonies or Plantations in *America*, or on the High Seas, or the Crime of Piracy, 17 Geo. 3, c. 9 (1777) (Gr. Brit.); 35 *Journal House of Lords* (1777) 78, 82–83 (Gr. Brit.) (noting royal assent given March 3, 1777).

George Washington, "Manifesto of General Washington, Commander in Chief of the Forces of the United States of America, in Answer to General Burgoyne's Proclamation," July 19, 1777, in *The Gentleman's Magazine, and Historical Chronicle for the Year 1777*, ed. Sylvanus Urban, vol. 47 (London: Printed at St. John's Gate, for D. Henry, 1777), 456–57; reprinted in *Continental Journal & Weekly Advertiser* 3, March 5, 1778 (Boston).

The Papers of Henry Laurens: December 11, 1778–August 31, 1782 15, ed. David R. Chestnut et al. (Columbia: University of South Carolina Press, 2000), 436 (replicating *Examination of Henry Laurens*, printed in *London Evening Post*, October 5–7, 1780).

David Duncan Wallace, *The Life of Henry Laurens* (New York: G. P. Putnam's Sons, 1915), 358–63, 388.

Daniel J. McDonough, *Christopher Gadsden and Henry Laurens: The Parallel Lives of Two American Patriots* (Selinsgrove, PA: Susquehanna University Press, 2000), 259.

An Act for the Better Detaining, and More Easy Exchange, of *American* Prisoners Brought into *Great Britain* of 1782, 22 Geo. 3, c. 10 (1782) (Gr. Brit.); 36 *Journal House of Lords* (1779–1783), 425–426 (London: 1767–1830) (Gr. Brit.) (noting royal assent given March 25, 1782).

Sheldon S. Cohen, *Yankee Sailors in British Gaols* (Newark, NJ: University of Delaware Press, 1995), 206.

John K. Alexander, *Forton Prison during the American Revolution: A Case Study of British Prisoner of War Policy and the American Prisoner Response to That Policy*, in *Essex Institute Historical Collections*, vol. 103 (Salem, MA: Essex Institute Press, 1967), 387.

Definitive Treaty of Peace, U.S.–Gr. Brit., art. 8, September 3, 1783, 8 Stat. 80.

Chapter 4

Tyler, *Habeas Corpus in Wartime*, 123–40.

Kevin Costello, *The Law of Habeas Corpus in Ireland* (Dublin: Four Courts Press, 2006), 6, 16.

Act of Settlement, 1701, 12 & 13 Will. 3, c. 2 (Eng.).

Journal of the General Assembly of South Carolina, Mar. 26, 1776–Apr. 11, 1776 (Columbia: Historical Commission of South Carolina, 1906), 21, 24, 26.

An Alphabetical Digest of the Public Statute Law of South-Carolina, ed. Joseph Brevard, vol. 1 (Charleston, SC: J. Hoff, 1814), 394 (reprint 31 Car. 2, c. 2 (Eng.)).

Ga. Const. of 1777, art. LX.

Charles Francis Jenkins, *Button Gwinnett: Signer of the Declaration of Independence* (Garden City, NY: Doubleday, Page, 1926), 109.

An Act to Punish Certain Crimes and Misdemeanors, and to Prevent the Growth of Toryism, ch. 20, § 12 (February 5, 1777), in *The Laws of Maryland*, ed. Virgil Maxcy, vol. 1 (Baltimore: Philip H. Nicklin, 1811), 338, 340–41.

An Act for the Better Securing the Liberty of the Citizens of This State, and for Prevention of Imprisonments (February 21, 1787), in *Laws of the State of New York*, ed. Thomas Greenleaf, vol. 1 (New York: Thomas Greenleaf, 1792), 369, 371–72.

James Kent, *Commentaries on American Law* 2 (New York. O. Halsted, 1827), 24.

U.S. Const. art. III.

The Records of the Federal Convention of 1787, ed. Max Farrand, vol. 2 (New Haven, CT: Yale University Press, 1911), 576.

"Report of Committee of Style," September 12, 1787, in *The Records of the Federal Convention of 1787*, 2:590, 596, 601.

The Debates in the Several State Conventions on the Adoption of the Federal Constitution, vol. 1, 148 (replicating Charles Pinckney's draft plan, art. VI).

An Act for Better Securing the Liberty of the Subject, 1781, 21 & 22 Geo. 3, c. 11, § XVI (Ir.).

Madison's Notes, August 28, 1787, in *The Records of the Federal Convention of 1787*, 2:438.

Alexander Hamilton, "The Federalist No. 83," in *The Federalist Papers*, 498–99.

Letter IV from the Federal Farmer to the Republican, October 12, 1787, reprinted in *The Documentary History of the Ratification of the Constitution*, ed. John P. Kaminski and Gaspare J. Saladino, vol. 14 (Madison: State Historical Society of Wisconsin, 1984), 42, 45.

Letter XVI from the Federal Farmer to the Republican, January 20, 1788, reprinted in *The Documentary History* 17, 348.

Ex parte Watkins, 28 U.S. (3 Pet.) 193, at 201–2 (1830) (Marshall, C.J.).

William Cushing, "Undelivered Speech," c. February 4, 1788, reprinted in *The Documentary History* 6, 1436.

U.S. Const. amend. V.

St. George Tucker, *Blackstone's Commentaries: With Notes of Reference, to the Constitution and Laws, of the Federal Government of the United States; and of the Commonwealth of Virginia*, vol. 1 (Philadelphia: William Young Birch and Abraham Small, 1803), app. at 292.

Letter from James Madison to Thomas Jefferson, October 17, 1788, in *The Writings of James Madison*, ed. Gaillard Hunt, vol. 5 (New York: G. P. Putnam's Sons, 1904), 272–74.

Chapter 5

U.S. Const. art. III.

Ex parte Bollman, 8 U.S. (4 Cranch) 75, 94, 95, 101, 135, 137 (1807).

Tyler, *Habeas Corpus in Wartime*, 141–56.

Proclamation of President George Washington, "Cessation of Violence and Obstruction of Justice in Protest of Liquor Laws in Pennsylvania," August 7, 1794, reprinted in *Claypoole's Daily Advertiser*, August 11, 1794.

Robert W. Coakley, *The Role of Federal Military Forces in Domestic Disorders, 1789–1878* (Washington, DC: US Army Center of Military History, 1988), 55.

William Hogeland, *The Whiskey Rebellion: George Washington, Alexander Hamilton, and the Frontier Rebels Who Challenged America's Newfound Sovereignty* (New York: Simon & Schuster, 2006), 215.

Act of April 30, 1790, ch. 9, §§ 1–2, 1 Stat. 112.

Message from President Thomas Jefferson to the Senate and House of Representatives of the United States, January 22, 1807, 16 Annals of Cong. 39 (1807).

Brian F. Carso Jr., *"Whom Can We Trust Now?"* (Lanham, MD: Lexington Books, 2006), 96–100.

Ex parte Burford, 7 U.S. (3 Cranch) 448, 452 (1806).

Act of February 12, 1793, ch. 7, 1 Stat. 302.

U.S. Const. art. IV, § 2.

Thomas Dean Morris, *Free Men All: The Personal Liberty Laws of the North, 1780–1861* (Baltimore: Johns Hopkins University Press, 1974).

Force Act of 1833, 4 Stat. 632 (1833).

Act of September 18, 1850, ch. 60, 9 Stat. 462.

Ableman v. Booth, 62 (21 How.) U.S. 506 (1859).

An Act to Repeal the Fugitive Slave Act of Eighteen Hundred and Fifty, and All Acts and Parts of Acts for the Rendition of Fugitive Slaves, ch. 166, 13 Stat. 200 (1864).

Act of February 5, 1867, 14 Stat. 385. Letter from Abraham Lincoln to Erastus Corning and Others, June 12, 1863, in *The Collected Works of Abraham Lincoln*, ed. Roy P. Basler et al., vol. 6 (New Brunswick, NJ: Rutgers University Press, 1953), 260, 264.

Chapter 6

Abraham Lincoln, "First Inaugural Address," March 4, 1861, in *Abraham Lincoln: Speeches and Writings, 1859–1865*, ed. Don E. Fehrenbacher (New York: Library of America, 1989), 215, 218.

Brian McGinty, *The Body of John Merryman: Abraham Lincoln and the Suspension of Habeas Corpus* (Cambridge, MA: Harvard University Press, 2011), 28.

"Affairs in Baltimore; Habeas Corpus Cask—Return of the Sheriff— Action of Chief Justice Taney—President's Instructions to Gen. Cadwallader, Suspending the Writ, etc.," *New York Times*, May 29, 1861.

Jonathan W. White, *Abraham Lincoln and Treason in the Civil War: The Trials of John Merryman* (Baton Rouge: Louisiana State University Press, 2011), 46–52, 59–60, 84, 92–95.

Tyler, *Habeas Corpus in Wartime*, 159–98.

Executive Order, August 8, 1862, in *A Compilation of the Messages and Papers of the Presidents*, ed. James D. Richardson, vol. 7 (New York: Bureau of National Literature, 1897), 3322.

Abraham Lincoln, Proclamation No. 1, 13 Stat. 730, September 24, 1862.

Abraham Lincoln, "Message to Congress in Special Session," July 4, 1861, in *The Collected Works of Abraham Lincoln* 4:421, 430.

Letter from the Attorney General to the Speaker of the House of Representatives, July 5, 1861, in *House of Representatives Executive Document No. 37-5* (1st Sess. 1861), 6.

Horace Binney, *The Privilege of the Writ of Habeas Corpus under the Constitution*, 2nd ed. (Philadelphia: C. Sherman & Son, 1862).

Horace Binney, *Second Part: The Privilege of the Writ of Habeas Corpus under the Constitution* (Philadelphia: John Campbell, 1862).

Letter from Abraham Lincoln to A. G. Hodges, April 4, 1864, in *The Collected Works of Abraham Lincoln* 7:281, 281.

Letter from Abraham Lincoln to Erastus Corning and Others, June 12, 1863, in *The Collected Works of Abraham Lincoln* 6:260, 264.

Act of March 3, 1863, ch. 81, § 1, 12 Stat. 755, 755.

Tyler, "Suspension as an Emergency Power," 655–62.

Proclamation No. 7, 13 Stat. 734, 734 (1863).

Proclamation No. 16, 13 Stat. 742, 743 (1864).

Mark E. Neely Jr., *The Fate of Liberty: Abraham Lincoln and Civil Liberties* (New York: Oxford University Press, 1991), 9, 30, 36–38, 44, 53, 130, 136, 160–84, 233–34.

Daniel Farber, *Lincoln's Constitution* (Chicago: University of Chicago Press, 2003), 20.

Andrew Johnson, A Proclamation, December 1, 1865; Andrew Johnson, A Proclamation, April 2, 1866; Andrew Johnson, A Proclamation, August 20, 1866, all reprinted in *A Compilation of the Messages and Papers of the Presidents*, 8:3531, 3627, 3631.

Ex parte Milligan, 71 U.S. (4 Wall.) 2 (1866).

Hamdi v. Rumsfeld, 542 U.S. 507 (2004).

Chapter 7

U.S. Const. amend. XIII, XIV, XV.

Robert J. Kaczorowski, *The Politics of Judicial Interpretation: The Federal Courts, Department of Justice and Civil Rights, 1866–1876* (New York: Oceana, 1985), 81.

Kermit L. Hall, "Political Power and Constitutional Legitimacy: The South Carolina Ku Klux Klan Trials, 1871–1872," *Emory Law Journal* 33 (1984): 921, 925.

Letter from Ulysses S. Grant to the Senate and House of Representatives, March 23, 1871, in *A Compilation of the Messages and Papers of the Presidents*, 9:4081.

An Act to Enforce the Provisions of the Fourteenth Amendment to the Constitution of the United States, and for Other Purposes, ch. 22, 17 Stat. 13 (1871).

Ulysses S. Grant, A Proclamation, May 3, 1871, in *A Compilation of the Messages and Papers of the Presidents*, 9:4088.

Charles W. Calhoun, *Conceiving a New Republic: The Republican Party and the Southern Question, 1869–1900* (Lawrence: University Press of Kansas, 2006), 31.

Robert W. Coakley, *The Role of Federal Military Forces in Domestic Disorders*, 310–12.

Ulysses S. Grant, A Proclamation, October 12, 1871; Ulysses S. Grant, A Proclamation, October 17, 1871; Ulysses S. Grant, A Proclamation, November 3, 1871; Ulysses S. Grant, A Proclamation, November 10, 1871, all reprinted in *A Compilation of the Messages and Papers of the Presidents*, 9:4089–95.

Tyler, "Suspension as an Emergency Power," 655–62.

Lou Falkner Williams, *The Great South Carolina Ku Klux Klan Trials: 1871–1872* (Athens, GA: University of Georgia Press, 1996), 19–39, 44–49, 53–61, 111, 122–25.

An Act to Suspend the Privilege of the Writ of Habeas Corpus in Certain Cases, Act of February 15, 1874, ch. 37, pmbl., Pub. Laws., 1st Cong., 4th Sess., in *The Statutes at Large of the Confederate States of America*, ed. James M. Matthews (Richmond: R. M. Smith, Printer to Congress, 1864), 187, 187.

S. Rep. No. 42-41, pt. 1, at 99 (1872).

Ex parte Yerger, 75 U.S. (8 Wall.) 85, 95 (1869).

Act of February 5, 1867, 14 Stat. 385.

Cong. Globe, 39th Cong., 1st Sess. 87 (1865).

William M. Wiecek, "The Great Writ and Reconstruction: The Habeas Corpus Act of 1867," *Journal of Southern History* 36 (1970): 530, 530–48.

Frank v. Magnum, 237 U.S. 309 (1915).

Moore v. Dempsey, 261 U.S. 86 (1923).

Carlos M. Vázquez, "Habeas as Forum Allocation: A New Synthesis," *University of Miami Law Review* 71 (2017): 645, 655–90.

Brown v. Allen, 344 U.S. 443 (1953).

Gideon v. Wainwright, 372 U.S. 335 (1963).

Brady v. Maryland, 373 U.S. 83 (1963).

Ford v. Wainwright, 477 U.S. 399 (1986).

Roper v. Simmons, 543 U.S. 551 (2005).

Stone v. Powell, 428 U.S. 465 (1976).

McCleskey v. Kemp, 481 U.S. 279 (1987).

Stone v. Powell, 428 U.S. 465 (1976).

Ann D. Gordon, *The Trial of Susan B. Anthony*, in *Federal Trials and Great Debates in United States History* (Washington, DC: Federal Judicial Center, 2005), 4–5.

Wainwright v. Sykes, 433 U.S. 72 (1977).

Teague v. Lane, 489 U.S. 288 (1989).

The Antiterrorism and Effective Death Penalty Act of 1996, Pub. L. No. 104-132, 110 Stat. 1214 (1996) (codified as relevant in Title 28 of the U.S. Code).

Harrington v. Richter, 562 U.S. 86, 103 (2011).

Williams v. Taylor, 529 U.S. 362 (2000).

Richard H. Fallon Jr., John F. Manning, Daniel J. Meltzer, and David L. Shapiro, *Hart & Wechsler's the Federal Courts and the Federal System*, 7th ed. (St. Paul, MN: Foundation Press, 2015), 1301–23.

Halliday, *Habeas Corpus*, 7.

Chapter 8

Densho website, *Terminology*, accessed October 1, 2020, https://densho.org/terminology/.

A. W. Brian Simpson, *In the Highest Degree Odious: Detention without Trial in Wartime Britain* (Oxford: Oxford University Press, 2005).

Peter Gillman and Leni Gillman, *"Collar the Lot!": How Britain Interned and Expelled Its Wartime Refugees* (London: Quartet Books, 1980).

Garner Anthony, "Martial Law, Military Government and the Writ of Habeas Corpus in Hawaii," *California Law Review* 31 (1943): 477, 478, 481–83, 486–92, 503, app. 1.

Hawaiian Organic Act of 1900, Ch. 339, 31 Stat. 141.

Duncan v. Kahanamoku, 327 U.S. 304 (1946).

Harry N. Scheiber and Jane L. Scheiber, *Bayonets in Paradise: Martial Law in Hawai'i during World War II* (Honolulu: University of Hawai'i Press, 2016), 263–84, 310.

Robert S. Rankin, "Hawaii under Martial Law," *Journal of Politics* 5 (1943): 270, 274–75.

Tyler, *Habeas Corpus in Wartime*, 211–43.

Exec. Order No. 9066, 3 C.F.R. 1092 (1942) (repealed 1976).

Letter from Attorney General Francis Biddle to Representative Leland Merritt Ford, January 24, 1942, reprinted in *Documents of the Committee on Wartime Relocation and Internment of Civilians* (Frederick, MD: University Publications of America, 1983), 5739, 5740, reel 5, 417–18.

Henry L. Stimson, Diary, February 3, 1942; Henry L. Stimson, Diary, February 10, 1942, Henry L. Stimson Papers, Yale University Library, reel 7, 85, 102.

Memorandum from Assistant to the Attorney General James H. Rowe Jr. to Grace Tully, Private Secretary to President Franklin Delano Roosevelt, February 2, 1942, in James H. Rowe Jr. Papers, Assistant to the Attorney General Files, Alien Enemy Control Unit, Box 33, Franklin D. Roosevelt Presidential Library, Hyde Park, NY.

Transcript of Telephone Conversation, Major Karl R. Bendetsen, Assistant to the Judge Advocate Gen., Major Gen. Allen W. Gullion, Provost Marshal Gen. of the U.S. Army, and Gen. Mark W. Clark, Deputy Chief of Staff of the Army Ground Forces, February 4, 1942, vol. 2, in *Documents of the Commission on Wartime Relocation and Internment of Civilians*, 5936, 5937, reel 5, 579.

Attorney General Francis Biddle, Memorandum, "Luncheon Conversation with the President," February 7, 1942, vol. 2, in Roosevelt, Franklin D. Correspondence Folder, Francis Biddle Papers, Box 3, Franklin D. Roosevelt Presidential Library, Hyde Park, NY.

Morton Grodzins, *Americans Betrayed: Politics and the Japanese Evacuation* (Chicago: University of Chicago Press, 1949), 19–94, 157–59, 255–73, 281–83, 358, 374.

Lt. Commander Kenneth D. Ringle to Chief of Naval Operations, "Report on Japanese Question," January 26, 1942, File ASW 014.311, RG 107, National Archives, Washington, DC.

Peter Irons, *Justice at War: The Story of the Japanese American Internment Cases* (New York: Oxford University Press, 1983), 19–59, 73, 102–3, 202–6, 278–92, 344–45.

Greg Robinson, *By Order of the President: FDR and the Internment of Japanese Americans* (Cambridge, MA: Harvard University Press,

2001), 2–7, 94–96, 100–106, 116–22, 171–72, 189, 214–21, 230, 234.

Hirabayashi v. United States, 320 U.S. 81 (1943).

Yasui v. United States, 320 U.S. 115 (1943).

Korematsu v. United States, 323 U.S. 214 (1944).

Trump v. Hawaii, 138 S. Ct. 2392, 2423 (2018).

Ex parte Endo, 323 U.S. 283 (1944).

Public Proclamation No. 21 (December 17, 1944), 10 Fed. Reg. 53–54 (January 2, 1945).

Commission on Wartime Relocation and Internment of Civilians, Personal Justice Denied, Part 1 (Washington, DC: Government Printing Office, 1982), 215.

Commission on Wartime Relocation and Internment of Civilians, Personal Justice Denied, Part 2: Recommendations (Washington, DC: Government Printing Office, 1983), 3, 5.

Amanda L. Tyler, "Courts and the Executive in Wartime: A Comparative Study of the American and British Approaches to the Internment of Citizens during World War II and Their Lessons for Today," *California Law Review* 107 (2019): 789, 813–26, 852–63.

R. (Miller) v. Secretary of State for Exiting the European Union [2017] UKSC 5 (appeal taken from Eng. and Wales).

Judith Farbey and R. J. Sharpe, *The Law of Habeas Corpus*, 3rd ed. (Oxford: Oxford University Press, 2011), 93.

Defence of the Realm (Consolidation Act) of November 28, 1914, 5 Geo. V, c. 8 (1914) (Eng.).

R. v. Halliday, [1917] A.C. 260.

Emergency Powers (Defence) Act of 1939, 2 & 3 Geo. 6, c. 62, 1(2)(a) (1939) (Eng.).

Defence Regulations 1939, Stat. R. & O. 1681, at 18B (Eng.).

Defence Regulations 1940, Stat. R. & O. 770 (Eng.).

Andrew Roberts, *Churchill: Walking with Destiny* (New York: Viking, 2018), 538.

War Cabinet, Memorandum of the Home Secretary, "Members of the British Union Detained under Regulation 18B," September 7, 1944, 2, CAB 66/55/5, National Archives (Gr. Brit.).

War Cabinet, Memorandum of the Home Secretary, "Should Detention Orders be Made under Defence Regulation 18B against Certain Persons Carrying on Prejudicial Propaganda," November 14, 1941, 1, CAB 66/19/40, National Archives (Gr. Brit.).

War Cabinet, Memorandum of the Home Secretary, "Accommodation
   for Married Couples Detained under Defence Regulation 18B,"
   November 21, 1941, 1, CAB 66/20/1, National Archives (Gr. Brit.).
A. W. Brian Simpson, "Detention without Trial in the Second World
   War: Comparing the British and American Experiences," *Florida
   State University Law Review* 16 (1988): 225, 241–42.
Note, "Civil Liberties in Great Britain and Canada during War,"
   Harvard Law Review 55 (1942): 1006, 1014–15.
"Mosley Speech," HO 45/24893/278, National Archives (Gr. Brit.).
Liversidge v. Anderson, [1941] 2 All. ER 612, 612–13 (C.A.).
Cable from Prime Minister Winston Churchill to Home Secretary
   Herbert Morrison, November 21, 1943; Cable from Prime Minister
   Winston Churchill to Deputy Prime Minister Clement Attlee and
   Home Secretary Herbert Morrison, November 25, 1943; Cable
   from Prime Minister Winston Churchill to Home Secretary
   Herbert Morrison, November 29, 1943, in Winston S. Churchill,
   The Second World War: Closing the Ring 5 (1951): 679, 680, 681.
Prime Minister Winston Churchill to Home Secretary Herbert
   Morrison, November 25, 1943, PREM 4/39/5, National Archives
   (Gr. Brit.).
Ivor Jennings, *The British Constitution*, 5th ed. (Cambridge:
   Cambridge University Press, 1966), 208.
Statement of James Madison, 1 Annals of Cong. 439 (1789).
Marbury v. Madison, 5 U.S. 137, 177 (1803).
Stephen Brooke, *Labour's War: The Labour Party during the Second
   World War* (Oxford: Clarendon Press, 1992), 37–38, 326–37.
Tom C. Clark, "Epilogue," in *Executive Order 9066: The Internment of
   110,000 Japanese Americans*, ed. Maisie Conrat and Richard
   Conrat, repr. ed. (Los Angeles: UCLA Asian American Studies
   Center Press, 1992), 110–11.

Chapter 9

Act of March 3, 1875, ch. 141, 18 Stat. 477 (1875) (repealed 1974).
Heikkila v. Barber, 345 U.S. 229, 235 (1953).
United States v. Jung Ah Lung, 124 U.S. 621 (1888).
Act of March 3, 1891, § 8, 26 Stat. 1085 (1891).
Nishimura Ekiu v. United States, 142 U.S. 651 (1892).
The Japanese Immigrant Case, 189 U.S. 86 (1903).
Act of September 26, 1961, Pub. L. No. 87-301, § 5, 75 Stat. 650, 651
   (formerly codified at 8 U.S.C. § 1105a(a) (1961) (repealed 1996)).

Hiroshi Motomura, "Immigration Law and Federal Court Jurisdiction through the Lens of Habeas Corpus," *Cornell Law Review* 91 (2006): 101, 459–69.

Pub. L. No. 104-208, div. C, 110 Stat. 3009-546 (1996) (codified in scattered sections of 8 U.S.C.).

Pub. L. No. 104-132, § 401(e), 110 Stat. 1214, 1268 (1996).

INS v. St. Cyr, 533 U.S. 289 (2001).

Zadvydas v. Davis, 533 U.S. 678 (2001).

8 U.S.C. § 1231(a)(6) (1994 ed., Supp. V).

Ireland v. United Kingdom, (1978) 2 Eur. Ct. H.R. (ser. B) 25, ¶¶ 81–84.

Act of 1971, c. 23, § 56(4) (Eng.).

Australian Government, Attorney-General's Department, National Security and Counter-Terrorism Law, Preventative Detention Orders, accessed February 1, 2020, https://www.ag.gov.au/NationalSecurity/Counterterrorismlaw/Pages/PreventativeDetentionOrders.aspx.

Terrorism Act, 2000, c. 11 (Eng.), as amended, Protection of Freedoms Act, 2012, c. 9, Pt. 4, § 57(1) (Eng.).

Terrorism Prevention and Investigation Measures Act, 2011, c. 23, § 1 (Eng.).

Counter-Terrorism and Security Act, 2015, c. 6, § 20(1) (Eng.).

Pub. L. No. 81-831, tit. II, § 102, 64 Stat. 1019 (1950) (repealed 1971).

81 Cong. Rec., 2d sess. 96, pt. 11, 15,632–15,633, 15,726 (1950) (reporting House and Senate votes on the Emergency Detention Act).

Zechariah Chafee Jr., "The Most Important Human Right in the Constitution," *Boston University Law Review* 32 (1952): 143, 160.

President Harry S. Truman, "Veto of the Internal Security Bill," September 22, 1950, accessed October 1, 2020, https://www.trumanlibrary.gov/library/public-papers/254/veto-internal-security-bill.

Louis Fisher, *Detention of U.S. Citizens* (Cong. Research Service, RS22130, April 28, 2005), 1.

Pub. L. No. 92-128, 85 Stat. 347 (1971) (codified in scattered sections of the U.S.C.).

18 U.S.C. § 4001(a).

Pub. L. No. 107-40, 115 Stat. 224 (2001) (codified at 50 U.S.C. § 1541 note (2006)).

Amanda L. Tyler, "The Forgotten Core Meaning of the Suspension Clause," *Harvard Law Review* 125 (2012): 901, 911–18, 1004–14.

Rumsfeld v. Padilla, 542 U.S. 426 (2004).

Padilla v. Hanft, 423 F.3d 386, 389 (4th Cir. 2005) (quoting Memorandum from President George W. Bush to Secretary of Defense Donald Rumsfeld, June 9, 2002).

Padilla v. Hanft, 546 U.S. 1084 (2006).

Padilla v. Hanft, 547 U.S. 1062 (2006).

Hamdi v. Rumsfeld, 542 U.S. 507 (2004).

Ex parte Quirin, 317 U.S. 1 (1942).

Hamdi v. Rumsfeld, 542 U.S. 507 (2004), opinion announcement (June 28, 2004), accessed October 1, 2020, https://www.oyez.org/cases/2003/03-6696.

Ex parte Milligan, 71 U.S. (4 Wall.) 2 (1866).

Daniel A. Farber and Suzanna Sherry, *Judgment Calls: Principle and Politics in Constitutional Law* (New York: Oxford University Press, 2009), 137.

Richard H. Fallon Jr. and Daniel J. Meltzer, "Habeas Corpus Jurisdiction, Substantive Rights, and the War on Terror," *Harvard Law Review* 120 (2007): 2029.

Trevor W. Morrison, "*Hamdi*'s Habeas Puzzle: Suspension as Authorization?," *Cornell Law Review* 91 (2006): 411.

Rasul v. Bush, 542 U.S. 466 (2004).

Tyler, *Habeas Corpus in Wartime*, 245–76.

Military Commissions Act of 2006, Pub. L. No. 109-366, 120 State. 2600 (2006) (codified in relevant part at 28 U.S.C. § 2241(e)).

U.S. Const. art. III, § 1.

Boumediene v. Bush, 553 U.S. 723 (2008).

Johnson v. Eisentrager, 339 U.S. 763 (1950).

Richard H. Fallon Jr., John F. Manning, Daniel J. Meltzer, and David L. Shapiro, *Hart & Wechsler's The Federal Courts and the Federal System*, 1238–40.

Halliday, *Habeas Corpus*, 7.

Jack Goldsmith, *The Terror Presidency* (New York: W. W. Norton, 2007), 110–20, 136–40.

Jonathan Hafetz, *Habeas Corpus after 9/11: Confronting America's New Global Detention System* (New York: New York University Press, 2011), 15–16, 185–87.

Lakhdar Boumediene, "My Guantánamo Nightmare," *New York Times*, January 7, 2012.

Ruth Wedgwood, "The Supreme Court and the Guantanamo Controversy," in *Terrorism, the Laws of War, and the Constitution:*

Debating the Enemy Combatant Cases, ed. Peter Berkowitz (Stanford, CA: Hoover Institution Press, 2005), 182.

Daniel J. Meltzer, "Habeas Corpus, Suspension, and Guantanamo: The *Boumediene* Decision," *Supreme Court Review* (2008): 2033–44, 2102, 2112.

Al-Waheed v. Ministry of Defence and Ministry of Defence v. Mohammed [2017] UKSC 2, ¶¶100–102 (opinion of Lord Sumption).

Rahmatullah v. Secretary of State for Defence (JUSTICE intervening) [2013] 1 AC 614.

Amanda L. Tyler, "The Counterfactual That Came to Pass: What If the Founders Had Not Constitutionalized the Privilege of the Writ of Habeas Corpus?," *Indiana Law Review* 45 (2011): 3, 13–20.

Department of Homeland Security v. Thuraissigiam, 140 S. Ct. 1959 (2020).

Amanda L. Tyler, "*Thuraissigiam* and the Future of the Suspension Clause," *Lawfare Blog*, July 2, 2020, https://www.lawfareblog.com/thuraissigiam-and-future-suspension-clause.

8 U.S.C. § 1225, 1252.

8 C.F.R. § 208.30(f).

Somerset v. Stewart, (1772) 98 Eng. Rep. 499 (K.B.), 1 Lofft 1.

Agency for International Development v. Alliance for Open Society International, Inc., 140 S. Ct. 2082 (2020).

Conclusion

Ex parte Milligan, 71 U.S. (4 Wall.) 2 (1866).

Liversidge v. Anderson, [1941] 2 All. ER 612, 612–613 (C.A.).

Israel Law Reports, H.C.J. 5100/94, September 6, 1999, 37.

1 William Blackstone, *Commentaries*, *126, *131, *133.

Further reading

Bailyn, Bernard. *The Ideological Origins of the American Revolution*. Cambridge, MA: Belknap Press of Harvard University Press, 1967. Reprint, expanded ed., 1992.

Baker, John. *The Reinvention of Magna Carta 1216–1616*. Cambridge: Cambridge University Press, 2017.

Blackstone, William. *The Oxford Edition of Blackstone's Commentaries on the Laws of England*. Edited by Ruth Paley. Oxford: Oxford University Press, 2016.

Care, Henry. *English Liberties, or the Free-Born Subject's Inheritance*. 5th cd. Boston: J. Franklin, 1721.

Coke, Sir Edward. *The Second Part of the Institutes of the Laws of England*. London: E & R Brooke, 1797. First published 1628.

Duker, William F. *A Constitutional History of Habeas Corpus*. Westport, CT: Greenwood Press, 1980.

Elliot, Jonathan, ed. *The Debates in the Several State Conventions on the Adoption of the Federal Constitution*. 2nd ed. Philadelphia: J. B. Lippincott, 1881.

Farber, Daniel. *Lincoln's Constitution*. Chicago: University of Chicago Press, 2003.

Farbey, Judith, and R. J. Sharpe. *The Law of Habeas Corpus*. 3rd ed. Oxford: Oxford University Press, 2011.

Farrand, Max, ed. *The Records of the Federal Convention of 1787*. New Haven, CT: Yale University Press, 1911.

Freedman, Eric M. *Making Habeas Work: A Legal History*. New York: New York University Press, 2018.

Goldsmith, Jack. *The Terror Presidency*. New York: W. W. Norton, 2007.

Grodzins, Morton. *Americans Betrayed: Politics and the Japanese Evacuation*. Chicago: University of Chicago Press, 1949.

Hafetz, Jonathan. *Habeas Corpus after 9/11: Confronting America's New Global Detention System*. New York: New York University Press, 2011.

Halliday, Paul D. *Habeas Corpus: From England to Empire*. Cambridge, MA: Belknap Press of Harvard University Press, 2010.

Irons, Peter. *Justice at War: The Story of the Japanese American Internment Cases*. New York: Oxford University Press, 1983.

Langbein, John H. *The Origins of Adversary Criminal Trial*. Oxford: Oxford University Press, 2003.

Larson, Carlton F. W. *The Trials of Allegiance: Treason, Juries, and the American Revolution*. New York: Oxford University Press, 2019.

McGinty, Brian. *The Body of John Merryman: Abraham Lincoln and the Suspension of Habeas Corpus*. Cambridge, MA: Harvard University Press, 2011.

Morris, Thomas Dean. *Free Men All: The Personal Liberty Laws of the North, 1780–1861*. Baltimore: Johns Hopkins University Press, 1974.

Neely, Mark E., Jr. *The Fate of Liberty: Abraham Lincoln and Civil Liberties*. New York: Oxford University Press, 1991.

Rakove, Jack N. *Original Meanings: Politics and Ideas in the Making of the Constitution*. New York: Vintage Books, 1996.

Rakove, Jack N. *Revolutionaries*. Boston: Houghton Mifflin Harcourt, 2010.

Rehnquist, William H. *All the Laws but One: Civil Liberties in Wartime*. New York: Vintage Books, 1998.

Robinson, Greg. *By Order of the President: FDR and the Internment of Japanese Americans*. Cambridge, MA: Harvard University Press, 2001.

Rossiter, Clinton, ed. *The Federalist Papers*. New York: Signet Classic, New American Library, 2003.

Scheiber, Harry N., and Jane L. Scheiber. *Bayonets in Paradise: Martial Law in Hawai'i during World War II*. Honolulu: University of Hawai'i Press, 2016.

Simpson, A. W. Brian. *In the Highest Degree Odious: Detention without Trial in Wartime Britain*. Oxford: Oxford University Press, 2005.

Tyler, Amanda L. *Habeas Corpus in Wartime: From the Tower of London to Guantanamo Bay*. New York: Oxford University Press, 2017.

Wert, Justin J. *Habeas Corpus in America: The Politics of Individual Rights*. Lawrence: University Press of Kansas, 2011.

White, Jonathan W. *Abraham Lincoln and Treason in the Civil War: The Trials of John Merryman*. Baton Rouge: Louisiana State University Press, 2011.

Williams, Lou Falkner. *The Great South Carolina Ku Klux Klan Trials: 1871–1872*. Athens, GA: University of Georgia Press, 1996.

Index